The Song Is Over

Fire Ant Books

Henny Brenner in Dresden in the courtyard of the Baroque Zwinger palace, early 1941.

The Song Is Over

Survival of a Jewish Girl in Dresden

Henny Brenner

Translated from the German with an Introduction
by Barbara Fischer

The University of Alabama Press
Tuscaloosa

Copyright © 2010
The University of Alabama Press
Tuscaloosa, Alabama 35487-0380
All rights reserved
Manufactured in the United States of America

Translated from *Das Lied ist aus: Ein jüdisches Schicksal in Dresden* published
by Pendo Verlag, Zürich 2001 (Neuauflage: ddp goldenbogen, Dresden 2005).
Copyright Pendo Verlag.

Translation Copyright The University of Alabama Press 2010.

Typeface: Caslon

∞

The paper on which this book is printed meets the minimum requirements of
American National Standard for Information Sciences-Permanence of Paper for
Printed Library Materials, ANSI Z39.48-1984.

Library of Congress Cataloging-in-Publication Data

Brenner, Henny, 1924–
  [Lied ist aus. English]
  The song is over : survival of a Jewish girl in Dresden / Henny Brenner ;
translated from the German by Barbara Fischer.
      p. cm.
"Fire Ant books."
  Originally published in German: Zurich : Pendo Verlag. 2001.
  Memoirs.
  Includes bibliographical references.
  ISBN 978-0-8173-5596-8 (pbk. : alk. paper) — ISBN 978-0-8173-8356-5 (e-book)
  1. Brenner, Henny, 1924- 2. Jewish women—Germany—Dresden—Biography.
3. Jews—Germany—Dresden—Biography. 4. Holocaust, Jewish (1939-1945)—
Germany—Dresden—Personal narratives. 5. Dresden (Germany)—Biography.
I. Title.
  DS135.G5B73313 2010
  940.53′18092—dc22
  [B]

                              2009032307

Contents

Illustrations

Acknowledgements

I would like to express my gratitude to the following individuals: Dan Ross for his immediate interest in and support of publishing this autobiography for an English speaking audience; Naomi Thurston and Steffi Ammons for their assistance during the initial translation phase; Reinhard Miller for his help with the index; Michael Brenner for his many suggestions; The University of Alabama's vice president for research, Joe Benson, and College of Arts and Sciences associate deans Jimmy Williams and Tom Wolfe for their generous financial support; Romy Proschmann for her competent assistance at the archives of the United States Holocaust Memorial Museum; and Cornelius Carter for his much-appreciated belief in and encouragement of this project. I extend heartfelt gratitude to my family, especially to Thomas Fox, who has given his time, patience, and indispensible help, from my initial conversations with Henny Brenner to the final proofreading phase. The translation is dedicated to our children, Katharina and Christopher, whose interest in Henny Brenner's autobiography has been considerable.

Introduction

While finishing some research in the archives of the United States Holocaust Memorial Museum in Washington, D.C., during the winter of 2009, I found a Nazi deportation table with names of Jewish citizens from Dresden, Germany. The list was assembled January 22, 1945. Next to number 204 I read: "Henny S. Wolf, born 11/25/1924 in Dresden." Next to number 205: "Sascha S. Wolf, née Katzenbogin, born 9/22/1890 in Minsk." The Nazis noted under "Comments" the letters "ef" (*einsatzfähig*), indicating that mother and daughter were considered "able or fit to work" at the designated camp.

As Henny Brenner, born Henny Wolf, tells the reader during the first pages of this, her autobiography, the deportation never took place. She and her mother received letters from the Secret State Police (Gestapo) of Dresden dated February 12, 1945. The Gestapo ordered both women to arrive promptly at 6:45 a.m. on February 16 at a given location to be sent to a "work assignment" outside Dresden. But the given location no longer existed on February 16. Between February 13 and 15, British and U.S. bombers had destroyed the city of Dresden.

Henny Brenner's autobiography starts with the obliteration of her hometown. The first sentence pulls in the reader with the powerful statement: "I owe my life to those fateful bombs that annihilated the city of Dresden during the night of February 13 to 14, 1945." Brenner, who had received her notice of deportation prior to the bombing, knew that a devastating attack would provide the only, and most unlikely, way to escape the camps. She was nearly twenty years old at the time. Her autobiography continues by reaching back to her memories of Dresden as a child, as a teenager, and as a young woman. Similar to Anne Frank, who would be a little younger than Brenner today,

Brenner tells the reader how she slowly lost all the privileges and plea-
sures a well-situated girl of her generation took for granted prior to
1933. Brenner, who had been raised Jewish by a Jewish mother and a
Protestant father, had been able to stay with her family until the air attacks as a result of her status. Children of so-called mixed marriages,
like Brenner, were sometimes able to avoid the worst through the ser-
endipity of having a non-Jewish parent, but, as this case shows, most
received a deportation notice at some later point.

In his afterword to the German edition of this book, Henny
Brenner's son, a historian, underscores the tragic irony that a human
being found liberation in a devastating inferno, an inferno occasioned
by one of the worst World War II bombing raids on a German city.
Originally a beautiful and elegant German city, Dresden was loved by
its citizens, whether the Nazis classified them as "Aryan" or "Jewish."
All survivors mourned the destruction of the city and the deaths of so
many innocent human beings. And yet, for those Jews not killed by the
bombs, the attack translated into salvation. How unbearable must the
fear and the horror of persecution have been for a human being to see
liberation in fire bombings?

Dresden lies on both banks of the Elbe River in the Eastern German state of Saxony. The Elbe valley, which reaches down to the Czech
border, creates a mild climate on the river. With moderate temperatures as well as Baroque- and Renaissance-style architecture, a famous
opera house, numerous world-renowned museums and art collections,
Dresden earned the "Florence of the North" sobriquet. During the
twentieth century the city experienced two dictatorships, that of the
Nazis from 1933 to 1945, and that of the East German Communists
from 1949 until 1989. Like her hometown, Henny Brenner experienced
hardships under both totalitarian regimes. She was part of the Dresden Jewish community during the Nazi regime, and her family did not
join the Communist Party after the liberation by the Red Army. Her
family rightly perceived a bleak future in East Germany and soon escaped to the West.

American readers will know of the bombing of Dresden through
Kurt Vonnegut's classic bestseller *Slaughterhouse-Five: Or The Children's Crusade*. The novel resulted from the author's own experiences
in Dresden. As an American POW in World War II, Vonnegut wit-

nessed the bombings and survived the horrific firestorm that destroyed the city. In February 1945, Dresden was overflowing with refugees from the Eastern front. The number of civilian casualties has been difficult to ascertain, but current historical research estimates 18,000 to 25,000 people died in the attacks. This figure has been an ongoing matter of dispute, and in Vonnegut's novel readers find a reference to U.S.A.F. Lieutenant General Ira C. Eaker estimating casualties reaching as high as 135,000. One of the more recent controversies took place in 2005, when a member of the German ultraright party, the NPD, went so far as to claim that half a million people died in the "bombing Holocaust." The Nazis, the East German Communists, and today's ultrarightists and neo-Nazis have used the Allied attacks to foment anti-British and anti-American sentiments among the Germans, but from the beginning there have also been more thoughtful antiwar voices such as Vonnegut's.

To this day, scholars debate whether the destruction of this major civilian and cultural center had military justification or whether the firebombing constituted a war crime. Jörg Friedrich's controversial book *Der Brand* (2002; *The Fire*, 2008) revived the discussion of the civilian and cultural costs of the Allied bombing campaign against Germany, with some readers warning of German revisionism and others welcoming a new debate on the use and abuse of airpower. In his study *Dresden: Tuesday, February 13, 1945* (2004), which refers to Brenner's autobiography, British scholar Frederick Taylor counters the view that the fateful destruction of the "Florence of the North" served no strategic purpose. He argues that, by the standards prevailing at the time, Dresden indeed constituted a justifiable military target.

The bombing of the city, followed by forty years of Communist neglect, changed the face of Dresden irrevocably. Official city planners as well as citizens and reconstruction enthusiasts, including British and American donors, have done much to rebuild or to support the rebuilding of the city in the post-Communist period. Nevertheless, tourists walking the streets of Dresden today still encounter World War II ruins and clunky Communist edifices as well as newer, postmodern architecture. These exist side by side with such restored Baroque treasures as the *Frauenkirche* ("Church of Our Lady"). This rebuilt cathedral symbolizes destruction and reconciliation, and it shares

the city skyline with the post-Communist architecture of such buildings as the new Jewish synagogue, built on the site where during the
"night of the broken glass" in November 1938 the Nazis burned the
synagogue designed by the famous Dresden architect Gottfried Semper. When Henny Brenner returns to "her" city today, little remains
from the Dresden she once called home.

Brenner's autobiography conjures up the unharmed Dresden of her
childhood. The reader comes to know the happy life of a girl growing
up in a middle-class household in the twenties and early thirties in one
of Germany's cultural centers. We find descriptions of life in the city,
family reunions in the countryside, visits with Jewish and non-Jewish
relatives, bourgeois preparations for theater evenings, and informative
recollections of doing laundry before electric washers and dryers. After
Hitler's rise to power in 1933, the autobiography focuses on the slowly
narrowing horizon of the girl's own private world. In 1933 Brenner
was eight years old. The Nazis categorized her as a so-called *Mischling*
(half-breed), that is, the offspring of mixed Jewish and non-Jewish
parentage. On September 15, 1935, the "Reich Citizenship Law" de-
fined citizens as "nationals of German or kindred stock." On November 14, 1935, the "Executive Order Pertaining to the Reich Citizenship
Law" proclaimed that "half-breeds with two full-Jewish grandparents"
could not be considered citizens of the Reich. The Hitler regime viewed
a "half-breed" with one "Aryan" parent more favorably than a "full Jew";
nevertheless, Brenner sensed, as she describes in her autobiography,
how her freedom diminished step by step. She encountered antisemitic
teachers at school. Her parents lost their spacious Art Nouveau apartment and had to move into much smaller lodgings. The Nazis categorized her father as "*jüdisch versippt*," a derogatory term for, in this
case, a non-Jew married to a Jew. He refused to divorce his Jewish
wife, and the Nazis confiscated his movie theater. After the pogrom
in November 1938, the persecution of Jews accelerated and the Nazis
closed Jewish schools. As a consequence, Brenner was never able to realize her dream of studying at an art academy. In July 1941 the Nazis
forced her into involuntary labor at a factory belonging to Zeiss-Ikon;
in 1943 she changed to the Bauer cardboard packaging factory. Beginning in September 1941 she had to wear the yellow "*Judenstern*," the
Star of David, an official sign of discrimination and humiliation. In

1945 the Gestapo interrogated her, and her parents feared she would not return alive.

Throughout the book the narrative does not describe physical violence against the author. Yet the reader witnesses Brenner's public stigmatization based on an artificial rubric of "race," and understands how this classification gradually destroys the dignity of an individual life. Unlike the scholarly Victor Klemperer, another Jewish survivor from Dresden who published his widely read diaries *I Will Bear Witness: A Diary of the Nazi Years* (1999; *Ich will Zeugnis ablegen bis zum letzten: Tagebücher 1933–1945*, 1995), Brenner had no ambition to be "a cultural historian of the catastrophe" (January, 10 1942). She recorded her experiences primarily for the inner circle of her family. Nonetheless, in published form Brenner's memories contribute to a neglected field of Holocaust research, that of life as a "half-breed," a *Mischling* in Nazi Germany.

The Wannsee Conference, where the Nazis outlined their "Final Solution to the Jewish Question," took place on January 20, 1942, outside Berlin. By the beginning of 1943, the Nazis had deported to the camps the majority of all German and Austrian Jews who had remained in their countries. "Halfbreeds" and partners living in "mixed" marriages, however, remained generally immune from deportation prior to the final phase of the war. Due to her "halfbreed" status, Brenner managed to remain in Dresden as a forced laborer. The Nazi leadership preferred to use *Mischlinge* and partners from "mixed" marriages as forced labor rather than deporting them and risking unrest from relatives in the "Aryan" population. Simultaneously, this measure provided tens of thousands of unskilled workers as cheap labor and also guaranteed strict control over individuals.

The census of 1939 shows that in the German Reich there were 20,454 registered "mixed" marriages. By the end of 1944, Jews living in these marriages and their children could no longer hope for protected status. But until that point, the fact that Brenner's Protestant father shared his wife's and daughter's humiliations throughout the Nazi period had shielded them from deportation as well as from starvation during the war years. The father's food ration cards, and his ability to travel to the countryside and obtain food from farms, became essential for the physical well-being and survival of mother and daughter.

Their Jewish status did not allow them to take public transportation or to ride bicycles, and their ration cards stamped with "J" did not provide sufficient nutrients. Their strongly bonded family life greatly increased the possibility of survival.

Nazi ideology regarding "race" appeared absolute and monolithic on the outside, but functionaries often handled individual cases in an arbitrary fashion within the regime. The question of how to categorize the children of Jewish and non-Jewish parentage, as well as the categorization of non-Jews married to Jews, became indeed quite complicated in practice. Such "racial" classification constituted an ongoing problem for Nazi authorities, in no small part due to the fact that Hitler remained reluctant to address the issue with a definite ruling. While the Nuremberg Race Laws of 1935 provided pseudoscientific guidelines and hierarchies concerning the definition of "Jewishness," the policies concerning "half-breeds" remained in flux, and the pendulum moved back and forth between integrating them with non-Jews or persecuting them as Jews. The Nazis attempted to stay attuned to the sensibilities of "Aryan" family members, and until the war years Hitler himself had insisted on maintaining control of issues concerning *Mischlinge*. The "Executive Order Pertaining to the Reich Citizenship Law" from November 14, 1935, which denied "halfbreeds with two full-Jewish grandparents" citizen status, also stated that the "Führer can grant exemptions from these regulations." We know that some individual cases were referred to Hitler personally, and that this practice continued during the war.

At first, deportations did not include "half-breeds" and Jews living in "mixed" marriages, but when the Nazis had completed the mass deportations of Jews of the German Reich in 1944, the circumstances of the "protected" groups changed drastically for the worse. Beginning in late 1944, Nazi operations reorganized their forced labor, deporting the laborers away from their home regions to distant camps. They now included Jewish "halfbreeds" and partners living in "mixed" marriages. Brenner's notification concerning her transport to a "work assignment outside of Dresden" arrived just prior to the bombings of Dresden. The fateful attacks saved her from deportation.

Until the bitter end of the "Third Reich," Brenner survived in hiding in the city. But after her liberation by the Red Army, she quickly learned that she also had to fear her liberators. As the Communists consolidated their power, Brenner and her parents realized that their refusal to join the Party doomed them once again to inferior status. Their situation deteriorated further in the early 1950s, as a wave of Stalinist-inspired antisemitism swept through the Soviet-bloc states, including East Germany. Fearing that Nazi-style persecution would begin again under the Communists, many East German Jews fled to the West, including Brenner's family. In December 1952, they found refuge in West Berlin. Henny Brenner was twenty-eight years old, a survivor of two totalitarian regimes as well as the infamous fire bombing of Dresden. Shortly after her arrival in the West, she married and moved to a Bavarian town, where she raised two sons and where she still lives today. Her parents died, many years ago now, of natural causes. During her lifetime she has experienced five different German governmental systems, stretching from the Weimar Republic to the current Berlin Republic. A frequent guest in today's postunification Dresden, Henny Brenner is one of the few living members of the former Jewish community of "her" city. She is the link to a Dresden as it was prior to Communist and Nazi dictatorships as well as prior to the apocalyptic destruction that saved her life.

Barbara Fischer

BIBLIOGRAPHY

Diamant, Adolf. *Chronik der Juden in Dresden: Von den ersten Juden bis zur Blüte der Gemeinde und deren Ausrottung.* Darmstadt: Agora, 1973.

Eckler, Irene. *A Family Torn Apart by Rassenschande: Politische Verfolgung im Dritten Reich. Dokumente und Berichte aus Hamburg.* Translated by Jean Macfarlane. Schwetzingen: Horneburg Verlag, 1998.

Fox, Thomas C. *Stated Memory. East Germany and the Holocaust.* Rochester: Camden House, 1999.

———. "Writing Dresden Across the Generations." In *Victims and Perpetrators: 1933–1945. (Re)Presenting the Past in Post-Unification Culture,* edited by Laurel Cohen-Pfister and Dagmar Wienroeder-Skinner. Berlin/New York: Walter de Gruyter, 2006, 136–153.

Friedrich, Jörg. *Der Brand: Deutschland im Bombenkrieg, 1940–1945.* München: Propyläen Verlag, 2002.

Gesellschaft für Christlich-Jüdische Zusammenarbeit Dresden e.V., Arbeitskreis Gedenkbuch, ed. *Buch der Erinnerung: Juden in Dresden: deportiert, ermordet, verschollen 1933–1945.* Dresden: Thelem Universitätsverlag, 2006.

Grenville, John A. S. "Neglected Holocaust Victims: The Mischlinge, the Jüdisch-versippte, and the Gypsies." In *The Holocaust and History: The Known, the Unknown, the Disputed, and the Reexamined*, edited by Michael Berenbaum and Abraham J. Peck, 315–326. Bloomington: Indiana University Press in association with the United States Holocaust Memorial Museum, 2002.

Gruner, Wolf. *Jewish Forced Labor under the Nazis: Economic Needs and Racial Aims, 1938–1944.* Translated by Kathleen M. Dell'Orto. New York: Cambridge University Press, published in association with the United States Memorial Museum, 2006.

Hatikva, ed. *Spurensuche: Juden in Dresden: Ein Begleiter durch die Stadt.* Hamburg: Dölling und Galitz Verlag, 1995.

Hecht, Ingeborg. *Invisible Walls: A German Family under the Nuremberg Laws. And: To Remember Is to Heal: Encounters between Victims by the Nuremberg Laws.* Translated by John Brownjohn and John A. Broadwin. Evanston: Northwestern University Press, 1999.

Jüdische Gemeinde Dresden. "Einsatzfähigkeit der Juden des Regierungsbezirks Dresden nach dem Stande vom 22. Januar 1945." *Dresden Jewish Community Records 1936–1948*, Microfilm, 35 mm., Reel 3. United States Holocaust Memorial Museum, 2001.

Klemperer, Victor. *Ich will Zeugnis ablegen bis zum letzten: Tagebücher 1933–1945*, edited by Walter Nowojski. Berlin: Aufbau Verlag, 1995.

Krüger, Helmut. *Der halbe Stern: Leben als deutsch–jüdischer Mischling im Dritten Reich.* Berlin: Metropol, 1993.

Lerm, Matthias. *Spurensuche: Juden in Dresden, ein Begleiter durch die Stadt mit sechs Karten.* Hamburg: Dölling und Galitz, 1995.

Meyer, Beate. *Jüdische Mischlinge: Rassenpolitik und Verfolgungserfahrung 1933–1945.* Hamburg: Dölling und Galitz, 1999.

Taylor, Frederick: *Dresden: Tuesday, February 13, 1945.* New York: Harper Collins, 2004.

Vonnegut, Kurt. *Slaughterhouse-Five: Or The Children's Crusade. A Duty-Dance with Death.* New York: Random House, 1969.

Walk, Joseph, ed. *Das Sonderrecht für die Juden im NS-Staat: eine Sammlung der gesetzlichen Maßnahmen und Richtlinien, Inhalt und Bedeutung.* Heidelberg/Karlsruhe: C.F. Müller Verlag, 1981.

The Song Is Over

I

Prelude in Hell

I owe my life to those fateful bombs that annihilated the city of Dresden during the night of February 13 to 14, 1945. What chain of events had occurred to cause a human being to breathe a sigh of relief in the midst of the most devastating disaster ever to befall a German city? What must have run through the mind of a twenty-year-old girl, who looked upon the destruction of her familiar childhood surroundings as the miracle of her own survival? I will attempt to tell this story, starting with that night that marked an important turning point for us and for the lives of all the inhabitants of Dresden.

For my family, and the approximately 170 surviving Jews in Dresden, this turning point looked a bit different than it did for the 100,000 people around us. For us, the night had lasted for twelve years; for the first time we now glimpsed dawn amidst the overwhelming suffering and misery. As did everyone else in those hours, I thought this is Dante's inferno on earth. And yet I knew that only in the midst of this inferno could we save ourselves. While the entire city was in mourning, we were rejoicing. Our house, too, had been bombed; we, too, feared we would be encircled by a wall of flames; we, too, froze at the sight of charred piles of bodies lying by the wayside. And yet, for the first time in years, we were free.

We, too, ran through a sea of burning houses, our last possessions tucked into a small backpack. The only difference was, besides the personal documents and photos, besides a few valuables and ration cards that had been stamped with a large "J," our backpacks hid something else: a yellow star[1] ripped from our clothing, and a gray deportation order. For the first time in over a thousand days, the yellow star that had repeatedly invited bystanders to hurl accusations and spit at us no longer clung to our breasts. A document dated February 12, 1945, the previous day, lay next to it in our backpack. The sender was the "Liaison of the Reich's Coalition of Jews in Germany for the district of Dresden." Next to my first name, Henny, stood the obligatory appendage Sara[2] and then the following words: "By order of the superior authority, the Secret State Police of Dresden, you are summoned to arrive at Zeughausstrasse No. 1, first floor on the right, promptly at 6:45 a.m. on February 16th, 1945. You must expect to be sent to a work assignment outside Dresden." Of course we knew that "work assignment" meant concentration camp. And we knew that we would not follow this order. Luggage and provisions, it was further stated, were to be brought along: "One suitcase or one backpack (not both) may be brought. Size and weight of the suitcase or backpack may not exceed the measurements of a piece of hand luggage. You will be expected to carry your own luggage for a longer stretch of the way." We had permission to take clothes, shoes, and a blanket; we couldn't take "stocks and bonds, currency, bank savings records, matches and candles."

"Only an attack can save us," my father said. We were determined to go into hiding. This plan would have had little chance of success, however, without the chaos triggered by the attack. What my father had uttered as a last desperate hope would prove true; to be sure, the bombing proved far worse than any one of us could have imagined. Some of the few remaining Jews from the once stately community of 6,000 members in Dresden could not rejoice in the attack. One of the so-called Jewish Houses in which the authorities had placed them also fell victim to the bombs; the Jews suffocated in the basement. We did not yet know this as we continued to fight our way through the streets, past the bombed bridges, and as we collapsed on the meadows lining the banks of the Elbe River. We heard that the Gestapo building was burning and cheered: "All of our files are destroyed!" We could hardly suspect that the Gestapo officers had previously removed our files and secured them. Even in these hours, when countless people were burning to death, they had nothing better to do than to track down the last Jews. Twelve years of terror had passed, but the worst three months were still to come.

2

The Mishpoche

The city that I saw burning had once served as a refuge to my grand-parents on my mother's side. They had left Russia in 1892, after the assassination of Czar Alexander II and the resulting anti-Jewish po-groms. They, the Katzenbogen family, had come with their six chil-dren by train from Minsk[1] to Dresden. Two families of friends, the Regenbogens and the Katzenellenbogens, preceded them. Regenbo-gen ("rainbow"), Katzenellenbogen ("cat elbow"), and Katzenbogen ("cat bow"): these names would provide many occasions for laughter in the family circle.

The given names provided the following generations with plenty to talk about. My mother, the youngest of the six Katzenbogen children, was actually called Schosche, a Yiddish nickname for Schoschana. "Schosche, they're shooting," her brothers had yelled as they had dragged her out of the house during a pogrom shortly before their departure. "Schosche" might be acceptable in the shtetl, but not in Germany. German bureaucrats therefore simply changed Schosche to Sascha—a male Russian name! This would later repeatedly draw offi-cials' attention and provoke questioning glances; when the Red Army liberated us in 1945, the name again caused suspicion. Sascha, born in Minsk; the immediate association was "You spy!" Her second name was Rebecca, but that was not enough for the family. Neither Rebecca, nor Schosche, nor Sascha were German enough. The family council met and decided that one needed a German name in Germany. After much debate, everyone agreed on "Frieda," a name unrelated to my mother's real name but especially popular at the time. In 1938, the Nazis decided this was still not enough, and the obligatory Sara was added to Schosche, Sascha, Rebecca, and Frieda.

Of course, my mother was not the only one whose name was Germanicized back before the Nazis demanded the biblical add-on. My aunt Anna had not been born with that name in Russia, she was named Chaje. Aunt Pauline's name was actually Pessel, her husband Max was Menasche, and such was the case for everyone in the family. Due to the fact that my grandmother was no longer alive when I was born, it would have been customary for me to be given her name. But Chane Gitel was out of the question in Dresden. So the family council, consisting of my mother Schosche, alias Frieda, my aunts Chaje, alias Anna, and Pessel, alias Pauline, met again. What was good enough for them was good enough for me. They changed Chane Gitel to Henny Kitty after a short but lively discussion. But we haven't even gotten to me yet.

My grandfather, who hailed from the tobacco trade, first worked in Dresden as a "tobacco tailor."[2] He then started a small cigarette factory, as did many Russian-Jewish immigrants, whose businesses boasted such exotic-sounding names as "Kasaky" or "Yramos," despite the fact that their owners were called Lande or Lewin in real life. The papirossi were still rolled by hand back then, and the ends that poked out were cut with a small hand machine.[3] My grandparents' business must have done well, for they lived in a large, comfortable apartment. A samovar stood in the living room; it was used throughout the day and served as a reminder of my grandparents' heritage.[4] They always drank tea. Apparently my mother, who was two years old when the family left Minsk, had always called out "Tschai" (tea) during the train ride and retained the word as one of the few Russian words she knew later on.

The grandparents were a *bekowete* (honorable) family, as they said in Jewish circles. Their life-style was traditionally religious, but not exaggeratedly pious. Theirs must have been a very hospitable home. Aunt Anna, the eldest of the six sisters, said there was constant coming and going in the apartment. Friends, mostly Russian emigrants, would ring at the front door without being expected, even late at night. They were always well received and generously fed. My grandmother's cooking was kosher, and if Cantor Hofstein (whose baritone voice was famous not only for his rendition of Sulzer's and Lewandowski's melodies in the synagogue, but also for his Schubert songs) can be believed, she made the best gefilte fish in Dresden. The long sideboard in the dining room was covered with warm and cold dishes the whole day; you could just help yourself to marinated herring, meatballs, salted pickles, honey cake, and many other specialties. Naturally all were homemade by my grandmother. If anything was missing in the spread, refills were soon brought from the kitchen. My mother later told me about many dishes she had eaten as a child but no longer knew how to cook. But she said she could still taste the flavor on her tongue. I was surprised how Grandmother managed everything with the help of one maid. She was, after all, raising six children. Sadly, all the photographs of my grandparents burned during the bombing, but I still remember in detail a brownish paper that showed my grandfather in a silk coat, with a fur-trimmed hat on his head.

On the day my mother first brought my future father home with her, my grandparents were not enthusiastic. He also came from a *bekowete* family and had had a good position at the Dresdner Bank for fifteen years.[5] But couldn't she find somebody Jewish? First one daughter had married a "Galician."[6] Galicians were not very popular with the Russian Jews, and now the youngest one came along with a goy, a gentile! They had met during an afternoon dance and tea party, events my mother still attended with her parents, as was conventional at that time. That must have been on the eve of the First World War. At those social events there was no separation according to religious denomination. They became a couple and stayed that way a long time, perhaps five or six years, before they married. This was partly due to the fact, as I mentioned, that her parents were hardly enthusiastic at the outset; furthermore, my father did not want to marry because of the war. Although he had been given a deferment from military service, he was afraid that they'd draft him later on, and he did not want to leave a widow behind. The Katzenbogens soon took to my father, especially after he announced voluntarily that he and my mother would raise their children Jewish. And so they did, although it was only one child. Religion was not important to my father, who had grown up in a liberal Protestant household. Back then nobody spoke about such things in our social circles. In 1920, when my parents married, for every two purely Jewish marriages there was one marriage between a Jew and a Christian. At that time my parents never suspected that the Protestant origins of my father would later save our lives. In retrospect, becoming

My parents, 1920

a war widow was the least of my mother's worries. Somehow my father managed not to be drafted through all the years of war. He hated
the military and detested the enthusiasm for the war during that time.
"I'm surely not going to put a gun in my hand and kill somebody," he
exclaimed to my mother, and he tried everything to avoid having to
serve. Before his first physical examination, he simulated heart prob-

lems by swigging an abundance of strong coffee right before it. He was temporarily deferred. Before the next physical examination, he disappeared for a time into the countryside and stayed with friends. We still have postcards to his mother and sister, in which he tells them he doesn't know when he can come back home again. In any case, he managed to remain a civilian until the end of the war. Before his marriage in 1920, he had quit his job at the bank and had (along with two partners) purchased two houses with a movie theater on Alaunstrasse.[7] That is to say, he actually bequeathed them as an engagement present to my mother in 1919. Only her name appears in the entry in the land register next to the other two (gentile) associates.

Four years after the wedding, I came into the world—feet first. I didn't make it too easy for my parents, even during the delivery. During those days, breech deliveries often ended badly, but the doctor, a woman on whom my mother had insisted (she absolutely didn't want a male gynecologist), managed without a hitch.

During that time we lived in an Art Nouveau-style apartment, close to the central park called "Grosser Garten." My first memories are of walks in the park, feeding the squirrels. I also remember our frequent family visits. My father took me with him to visit his mother quite often; she lived above our movie theater in an attic apartment. She lived there rent free, that goes without saying, since her son was her landlord. She was a woman with a kind heart who used to give presents to everyone—especially to me, her only grandchild. My father also had a sister, but she never married or had children. When I would go up to my grandma's place, the smell of her cooking—liver, mashed potatoes, and brown onions—filled the stairwell. A special treat for me was feeding the finch in the birdcage; I was allowed to feed him lettuce leaves and birdseed. Grandma also got along well with my Mama. After the wedding there was no tension on either side because of the different religions. My father's sister, Aunt Grete, was also involved with a Jew, but later couldn't marry him because of the Nuremberg Race Laws.[8] Uncle Leo, as I called him, had a factory that produced casket blankets, which made him a not-so-small fortune. For him, however, there would be no casket blanket, not even a casket. Grete could offer no protection to Uncle Leo because they were not married, unlike my parents. The Nazis deported him and he was probably gassed at Ausch-

My mother (left), our nanny Eia, and I in Grosser Garten

witz. Aunt Grete was strikingly beautiful and I loved her deeply. Several rumors circulated about her: how a Count had ruined himself for her, amassed gambling debts, and then put a bullet through his head. She left Dresden after that; my father was upset and "pushed her away." But we didn't talk much about that. I often spent my school vacations with her in Berlin. We went to the Wannsee[9] and went shopping in the huge KaDeWe department store.[10] One time she cooked "green eel." I can still see it in front of me—how she lifted the lid and the brute jumped at her. She screamed horribly, and my father poured the entire content of the pot into the toilet.

My paternal grandparents' silver wedding anniversary with Aunt Grete and
my father

My mother's family was bigger than my father's. Not all her siblings stayed in Dresden; two of her brothers went abroad. Uncle Willy
went to England where he started a family—I only got to know them
through pictures and letters. To make up for that, we were always
in contact with my mother's other brother, Uncle Max, who, while
searching for a job, landed in Denmark. He worked in Copenhagen
as a jeweler. I met him once when he visited us, accompanied by my
cousin Esther shortly before the outbreak of the Second World War.

My mother also had a huge family in Dresden. Every week I would
go with my mother to Aunt Pauline's. Her husband Max (Menasche
actually) Rauch had a clothes store, a "Kluftengeschäft:" "Hojsen"
(pants) and "Marinarkes" (jackets), as they say in Yiddish. It was located on Große Brüdergasse, behind the Postplatz.[11] It was not really
a shop but an arched vault in the basement. It always smelled musty
and I didn't like to go in. Uncle Max was a good fellow but had one big
fault: he came from Galicia, and my grandparents did not like that one
bit. The "Litwakes," as the Jews from White Russia and Latvia were
called, looked down on the "Galicians." They also disliked the "Yekes,"

The Rauch family: Cousin Alfred, Aunt Pauline, Uncle Max

the assimilated Jews from Germany. But the Rauchs were not poor; Uncle Max did quite well with the "Hojsen." Papa often did a comic impression of my uncle's sales techniques: when the "Jacketel" did not fit right, Max pushed the customer in front of a mirror. The jacket was then gathered in the back, so it looked like it fit in the front; then the customer was turned around quickly, and it was gathered in the front, so it looked like it fit in the back. Papa also claimed that they put a German mark piece in the pocket of the jacket—not a small amount of money at that time. When provincial customers reached into the pocket during the fitting, they decided to buy the jacket in a hurry. Naturally this one mark had already been added to the price. I doubt that all of that was true, but my father did not put it past Uncle Max. During the "good times," my father was often upset because Uncle Max was such a cheapskate. They never rented a proper apartment but lived right above their shop in the cellar vault. When you opened the door of the apartment, you were right in the kitchen. My aunt was not tall, and when I came over, she quickly climbed on a footstool, opened the top door of the brown kitchen cabinet and got a small piece of chocolate for me. Then she put the rest back, locked the cabinet carefully, and hid the set of keys in the pocket of her apron. My father always complained that they couldn't even give me a whole chocolate bar. There was a long hall behind the kitchen that led to my Cousin Alfred's room. Some kind of light came from there that I considered creepy. My father never visited the Rauchs' apartment but did join us (for my mother's sake) when we took our Sunday trips with them. Most of the time, we took the tram route 11 to the hilly district of Bühlau and hiked through the forest to the inn called "Totenmühle."[12] They had a beer garden with long tables that were arranged underneath large, old chestnut trees. Customers ordered malt beer in high glasses with long wooden spoons. There were always a lot of bees, and I thought the purpose of the wooden spoons was to swat the bees. Everyone would bring their own sandwiches. This was allowed and was the reason the Rauchs always went there. My father sat there sulking, and I was bored. My cousins, Alfred and the son of a sister of Uncle Max, annoyed me constantly. For me, the best part of the whole trip was the long tram ride.

Alfred was the pride of the family. He went to a prep school and later studied dentistry. During the Nazi period, he went to Berlin to the Charité Hospital,[13] and when the authorities didn't allow him to work there anymore, he went to the Jewish hospital. His parents bought him a complete set of dental equipment that we later hid in our basement. I can still see the cases in front of me; they fell victim to the bombs. But by that time, the Rauchs, together with Alfred, had already been deported to Auschwitz. We never heard from them again.

We spent most of our time with my cousin Paula, who was eighteen years older than I, and with her mother, Aunt Anna. She married Jakob Goldberg, who was originally from the area around Kalisch.[14] He worked in the tobacco industry, too. After getting married, Anna went in search of work, first to Holland and then to England. There were a lot of tragedies in their family. A relative, Willy Goldberg, died at the very beginning of the First World War, not long after signing up as a young volunteer. His name is the first one on a memorial for fallen soldiers of the First World War that can be seen today in the Jewish cemetery in Dresden. Anna had returned to Dresden, because her husband had died young from a heart attack in Manchester, where they had moved shortly before. She returned to Dresden with little Paula and Willy, who was three years older than Paula; another child had died of diphtheria. Anna relied on family members for support. They moved into the large, old apartment of my grandparents on Dürerstrasse. I remember a long, narrow corridor, a special room with a green plush sofa and a small table. On it stood an old gramophone with a horn and a hand crank. Later on Paula worked for the popular Jewish fashion house *Rehaut* on Pragerstrasse. There she waited on the mother of Richard Tauber,[15] and the mother of Wilhelm Furtwängler.[16] Mr. Rehaut always greeted her erroneously as "Mrs. Furchtwängler" and told her about his excursions to the "Wannensee." In the beginning, Nazi big shots shopped there: the wife of the later district leader Mutschmann, and the wife of Baldur von Schirach.[17] They preferred to be assisted by Miss Goldberg; later on, however, this did not help her much. First the Rehauts were forced to move to a small side street, then they left the country for Argentina. They ended up being close to my cousin Paula who had gone to Bolivia. Back before the war, however, Paula didn't even know where Bolivia was.

3
Childhood Impressions

My parents lived a typical middle-class life. We moved from the apartment near Grosser Garten to a small villa in the Deutsche Kaiserallee, which nowadays bears the more agreeable name of Mendelssohnallee.[1] The owners of the house were two old spinsters and their brother. They lived above us. The slightly retarded brother handled the tasks of a caretaker, swept the street, worked in the garden, and picked fruit for me from the trees, even when it was not yet ripe. I ate it, of course, got a stomachache, and on top of that got scolded.

Dr. Ibner lived across the street. He was a real character who always wore woolen, knee-length socks, knickerbockers, and carried a big, brown, scraped-up midwife's bag. He only rode a bike to his patients. My father and Ibner often sat together in the study and took a nip or two. The study consisted of a large, brown leather sofa, deep armchairs, and a round table with a green marbled top and carved legs. There was also a bookshelf and a desk—all in richly carved dark wood. Mama did not like Dr. Ibner; he was too uncouth for her. An adherent to the health regiment developed by Sebastian Kneipp,[2] he wanted to toughen me up, because I always was so pale that people called me the "moonlight princess."

My Mama insisted that I drink my milk from a baby bottle for a rather long time. She thought that this way she would know how much I was drinking. If anyone would know about such things, it would be her, for according to one of our most beloved family stories, she was still breastfed by her mother at the age of two. She would take a little footstool and climb by herself up to her mother's breast. The fact that I still drank from the bottle when I was already attending elementary school was shameful. Years later they told me that I always lay fully dressed on the chaise longue sucking on my baby bottle with my school satchel next to me. One morning our doorbell rang and the maid opened the door without me noticing it. It was a school friend who came to pick me up. When she saw the bottle next to me, I was terribly ashamed, and I refused for a long time to drink milk at all. I preferred to give it to the small, half-starved cats that I brought home with me. Or I took money from my piggy bank to buy them ground meat that they polished off in no time at all. Then I utilized all my powers of persuasion in order to get the maid to go again and buy something. Early in the morning the cats were always gone, for my father would take them into the back yard. That was because during the night they would nibble on the beautiful cane furniture in the hall.

My little stuffed bear sat on an armchair in the hall. I didn't like to play much with dolls. But there was one I carried with me, a very old one that my grandfather had won for my cousin Paula in the lottery. It still had ball and socket joints and threw its arms far into the air. My father called her the machine gun, and I was deeply offended. Furthermore, the nose had broken off her ceramic face. I was not allowed to take her into my bed with me. So I slept with my bear Jumbo that my cousin Willy had won at the Dresden Vogelwiese. The Dresden Vogelwiese was a kind of an Oktoberfest. I wasn't thrilled by the thought of going there, but I was a little curious about it. My Papa took me on his shoulders, so that I would not get stepped on. There was a ghost train, a Ferris wheel, swinging boats and hurdy-gurdies, sticky Turkish honey, and barrels with pickled gherkins. I wanted to eat them, but was not allowed to, because my father was convinced that the vendors would wash their hands in the barrels.

My father was totally unable to provide for himself alone at home, which was typical for men at that time. My mother told me that once when she was away for a few days, and the maid was not there, he put all the dirty dishes into the bathtub, and filled it up to the top. That was his way of washing the dishes.

On Sundays Papa often took me with him to the park, to Grosser Garten, because the maid had the day off, and Mama cooked. Mama never let the help cook for us on other days, either. We passed the time riding in a horse-drawn carriage. Papa had bought newspapers, and we

My father and I at Pirnaischer Platz

went to Pollender, the coffee house. There we had a second breakfast of bouillon soup and a flaky pastry, a vol-au-vent. Across the way, in the Palaisteich,[3] we would feed the swans. Then we would make our way back home. I was terribly proud to be allowed to walk in Grosser Garten with my father. I could never walk quietly. I was constantly falling into puddles or onto sharp pebbles. Once, when my father did not want to go back with the carriage, I threw myself into the sand in my Sunday dress, and I started to scream. I still remember how people walked by and called to my father with an indignant look: "I would give her a good spanking." My Papa did not do this, of course. On another occasion, I was in search of a shell in a pond that had been drained. I got stuck up to my ankles in mud. My red shoes remained buried in the mud and I had to walk home barefoot. When we lived in Blasewitz,[4] I loved to ice-skate in the Waldpark.[5] You had to screw the blades onto the shoes with a special tool. Our parents would hang it around our neck, because if you lost it, you couldn't get the things off again. This happened once to a friend of mine. Older women rode on the ice with "chair-sleds," real chairs with blades attached. There was a little house that served mulled wine and sweets, like "Nabos," a kind of Turkish honey with chocolate icing. The "Petersburg Nights" were especially pretty. During this time, the skating rink was illuminated, there was music, and we danced waltzes.

4

Laundry Day

The laundry days are among my most lasting childhood memories. Laundry day occurred once every four weeks. Back then you did not wash clothes twice a week. There were no electric washing machines but instead one with two legs called the laundry woman. She had a fixed appointment with her clients, and came, depending upon the agreement, once a month from Hosterwitz, a suburb of Dresden. In the summer, her husband drove the cart back in the evening, because she stayed the whole day to do the laundry. In the winter, when the laundry couldn't dry outside, sometimes she would take it home and bring it back clean and dry. Most of the time, though, we dried it in our attic. There you could see stiffly frozen men's underwear and bed sheets, congealed to boards, hanging on the clothesline. My father called the laundry woman the "iron horse," because she was big and strong like the mythical Bavaria. She put up her blond hair in a bun and had hands like a loaf of soldier's bread. She had red cheeks and a full bosom. For starters, she was served breakfast. Our maid did that with a grumpy countenance, because she found it beneath her dignity to serve the laundry woman. The rest of the day, the maid ran around in the kitchen with large coffee pots, made of stoneware, and huge piles of sandwiches, and shouted to the laundry woman to come upstairs. On laundry day we always had stew for lunch. I was probably the one who was the most excited, and I had already prepared everything: my dolls' dresses, my teddy's clothes, and a tiny wooden tub with a small washboard. I was constantly pushed back and forth and got in everybody's way. They tied a blue apron around me, and I received a thousand admonitions regarding this dangerous undertaking. The maid, "Eia" (actually, her name was Elisabeth), also helped in the laundry

room. She did it unwillingly, and always accompanied by loud bicker-
ing with the "iron horse," who in the end always won their arguments.
The whole house reeked of curd soap, and when you went down the
stairs to the basement, the steam came into your face. Opening the
door of the laundry room was a risk. I would stand there in my small
wooden clogs, hair pinned up, and loaded heavily with my tub, washboard, and the dolls' clothes. Eia, who was otherwise always very nice
to me, growled at me. That did not bother me at all, since I was allowed
to participate in the activities. My Papa preferred not to come home on
laundry days. He always had to handle "important business" in the city.
It was bad enough—as far as he was concerned—that the soap smell
was still in the house in the evening.

The washing process was like a holy ritual, and woe if the maid
messed something up. For days beforehand, my mother and Eia
searched for everything washable. Mountains piled up in the laundry room. On the evening before, the laundry was prepared for soak-
ing overnight in huge tubs with cold water and a special detergent.
The first step was to wring out the pieces thoroughly, then to fluff
them, and then to throw them into the water, which was boiling in a
big kettle, called the boiler. Eia would heat it up for one hour in the
laundry room. The soap powder was already in the water. Especially
dirty areas had to be preprocessed; we scrubbed collars and cuffs with
curd soap. The boiler sat in a square-shaped stone oven. Near the bottom you could open a door to stoke the fire for the boiler. The laundry bubbled and steamed for perhaps half an hour. We couldn't let
the fire in the boiler go out even in high summer temperatures. Then
came the most dangerous part: the laundry had to be fished out with
two long wooden spoons—they always seemed to me like oars. During that procedure, Eia literally pulled me out of the laundry room. I
think that she was glad to have an excuse to leave the room. The boiling water could have splashed, after all. But the "iron horse" was always
careful and developed a skillfulness that you would not have expected
from this colossus. There was never an accident. After the laundry
cooled, it could be processed. First, it was spread out on the washboard, which was standing in a tub. On the top of the board there was
a holder for the curd soap and the brush. Then the real work would
begin. The laundry woman lathered, scrubbed, and then held the laun-

dry up against the light to check if it was clean, piece by piece, inside and out, one side and the other side. First she washed the underwear, then the bed sheets, then tablecloths. Not everything fit in the boiler at once, so the procedure had to be repeated. The soapy water was not poured out; it was recycled for the dark clothes. The water did not need to boil that much for the hot washing of aprons and other dark pieces. Socks were also washed right away by hand in the soapy water.

Most important was the rinsing. After the scrubbing, the laundry was thoroughly wrung out. None of us were able to do that, only the laundry woman. She wrung and wrung the laundry so strongly that ultimately, not a drop of water was left in it. Then, to get the soap out, it was boiled again in big tubs, rinsed twice with hot water and a few times with cold water. Afterwards, it was wrung out again and again. At the end, Mama came into the laundry room and felt every piece to see if there was any soap left in it. One knew already back then that leftover soap was not good for the skin.

In the meantime, I had strongly scrubbed my dolls' clothes. Unfortunately, they could not withstand my cleaning methods and we had to buy new ones. Of course, I was always very wet after all the scrubbing and cleaning; Eia dragged me upstairs, with a lot of nagging and screaming, to take off my wet clothes. She was only successful by promising me that I could go to the meadow next to the house where the laundry was bleached. Laundry that was still stained would be carried in baskets to the meadow, where it was spread out in the sun. Strangely enough, on laundry day, the sun was almost always shining, at least in my memory. The laundry was generally still wet, but was watered again. Then I jumped around with my bare feet on the laundry. Afterwards, it was put in the boiler again, and was boiled a second time. Probably it had green stains from the grass.

By around three o'clock in the afternoon everything had been washed; it was our job to hang the laundry on clotheslines. My mother also helped with it. The "iron horse's" husband picked her up in the horse cart. On the cart there were always numerous laundry baskets from people who sent their laundry to Hosterwitz and got it back later, because they had no laundry room or no place to dry the wash.

Finally, the first pieces were hanging on the line. I wore a small apron with clothespins and had a footstool, so that I could reach the line. They allowed me to hang up small pieces on my own. I would be severely scolded, however, if I dropped something on the grass, or stepped on an edge. We were happy when the laundry dried in one day. Entertaining for me, but terrible for the others, was when a thunderstorm or a summer shower were imminent. If storm clouds gathered, we ran outside and squinted up into the sky—the maid with a prayer, and me hoping for the first drops. We carried the already dried pieces of laundry inside to be on the safe side. A calm waiting period followed, the silence before the storm: no wind, no birds chirping, and we stood by quietly. At the first rustling of the trees, we rushed into the garden, tore the laundry from the line, while the first heavy raindrops were already splattering down. I was very worried about my dolls' clothes, and, of course, I got in everyone's way. If we were lucky, the sun was shining again after half an hour, and the whole process started over again. My Mama hated it when this happened. She was very picky and when hanging up laundry, one had to pay attention to many things: under no circumstances should we overstretch the corners, we should smooth and straighten everything by hand, and we shouldn't put the clothespins on the corners. If we had bad luck, it would continue to rain.

Once our boiler broke, shortly before our regular appointment. The "iron horse" had to take the laundry home with her. My mother couldn't stand that. She didn't know what kind of other laundry it would be mingled with, what soap the laundry woman would use, and if she would rinse often enough. Everybody said afterwards that the laundry was grey. I wanted, by all means, to see for once what really happened in Hosterwitz, and pestered my Mama all the time. She finally gave in, and I was permitted to go to Hosterwitz with the maid by tram over the Blaues Wunder bridge[1] for twenty pennies. That was an adventure! When we arrived, we found ourselves at a farm with some animals. The husband ran the farm, the wife the laundry business. There were huge tubs for bleaching and drying the laundry, and mountains of wood and briquettes were piled up outside. I was allowed to see everything, but preferred to spend most of the time with the animals in the stable. The best part was the ride back. Since the laundry had to be delivered, I was allowed to go along on the horse cart. The maid was not enthusiastic about this idea and would have preferred to go by tram. The cart was fully loaded with baskets, all tightly fastened, and I sat in the middle on the coach-box. The cart ride began, literally over sticks and stones; the roads were uneven in the countryside. We all sang in the wagon: "The sausage man came running fast down Blase-witzer Street. Why running, gasping, you might ask? Was snatching all the meat." The laundry woman was singing the loudest. And her sing-ing was not all that bad, as even my mother admitted, who had a good ear and understood a great deal about music. I wanted to hold the reins by all means, and thus arrived at home well shaken, where Mama al-ready stood waiting in front of the garden gate.

After the drying and delivery of the laundry, the whole process was not yet finished, since the laundry was still not "closet-ready." The next day, the work continued. We had to stretch the laundry and also sprinkle it briefly with water if it was entirely dry. Finally, we stored everything in the wash baskets and in the process we sprinkled it again and again, because it had to remain a bit damp until the third day. Then it was taken to be machine ironed, or, as we used to say in Saxony, the laundry came on the roller. The place was not far away from our house; we could bring it there with the handcart. The maid pulled it, Mama held the baskets. We walked on the road, because in our area there was little traffic, no tram, and there were not yet many cars. The mangle was already electric, nevertheless, the maid sang: "Come, let's turn the roller, you are so strong, so firm. Oh, don't be shy and don't ask why, the handle let's both turn." She sang of course, in the most beautiful Saxon dialect. Mama looked at us with consternation. When, back at home, we finally had the laundry sorted, had tied it with pink and light blue satin bands, and had stored it in the high closets, I heard my mother call out "Baruch Haschem" (Thank God).

5

At the Theater

The monthly theater visits were more pleasant for my parents. They had subscriptions for the opera and the theater. Every visit needed careful preparation. The seamstress came to our house two weeks in advance. I remember her as an old, dried-out spinster. She came in the morning at nine and stayed until the evening. However, she did not sew anything new for Mama: she clearly did not have enough fashion sense. Mama only let her make some alterations and repair some clothes. She bought her elegant clothes only in the Prager Strasse.[1] The workplace of our seamstress was a back room with an old sewing machine from "Seidel & Naumann," a popular Dresden company. The machine rumbled terribly. The maid had to make coffee and sandwiches again, but this time she did it in good spirits. That was because she would get something sewn for her from some of the leftover cloth, which we gave to her as a present.

When the clothes were ready and Papa's dark suit was laid out, the hairdresser would come to the house at noon. She also manicured Mama's nails. There was no nail polish at that time, but she rubbed a sweet-smelling powder or paste into the nails, and then polished them with a long polisher. Mama couldn't wash her hands afterwards; otherwise everything would have come off. When Mama's hair was styled, I wasn't allowed to come too close to her. But my father, when he came home, always took her head in his hands and gave her a big kiss. She screamed each time: "But Max, my hair!" She put on the dress, or better, the evening gown, at the end. This, of course, took time. The stockings back then had a seam on the back and it had to be exactly straight; otherwise one appeared to have "crooked legs."

The Dresden Opera, designed by Gottfried Semper, who also designed
the synagogue

I stayed at home with the maid who prepared my dinner before
my parents left. They did not eat at home on those days, but after the
performance they went to the theater restaurant or to the Dresdner
Rathskeller,[2] where they were regular guests. They always took a taxi
on these nights. I was supposed to try to go to sleep before they left
the house. You think so! Once more before she left, my mother tiptoed
to my door, which was not easy in her high heels. At that moment, I
would shout: "Mama!" She came back again, sat down all dressed up
next to the bed, and said she would come back soon, which was not
true. She would calm me down, tell me Eia would be there, and try to
speak to me while my father was in the hallway impatiently urging her
to hurry lest they be late. Other times, when I just did not want to go
to sleep and relatives were visiting, my father took me on his shoulders
after I was already washed up. He carried me through the apartment
while singing "tarramtamtam, tarramtamtam"; behind us my cousin
Paula walked with my teddy or my Moorish doll on the arm, then be-

Our movie theater, the "Palace Theater," in the Alaunstrasse, 1935

hind them, my grandma with the "punch bowl" in her hand. This was a white, heavy, porcelain chamber pot. I didn't want this spectacle to end, and bawled when my father wanted to transport me into bed.

Sometimes I was also allowed to go to the theater, to the fairy tales performed in the afternoon. Generally these took place around Christmas. I had to wear my pretty blue velvet dress with a white lace collar, and patent leather shoes and terribly scratchy wool tights. I hated to be dressed up like a fashion doll. But Mama attached great importance to such things. My father had also brought her the latest child stroller from the Leipzig trade fair. When my parents did their shopping with it, dressed elegantly, friends called us the "elegant team."

I went to the movies more often than I went to the theater, because it did not cost anything for me to go. A movie theater back then was something very new, and for a child, having a papa who owned one was at least as awesome as if he owned a toy store. I could always take my girlfriends along to our movie theater. The movie theaters back then were quite elegant; one tried after all to imitate theaters. Our cinema was called "Palace Theater." People came into the entrance hall through a portal with columns, passing by a uniformed doorman, and then walked up the stairs into the hall. The seats and curtains were made of red velvet. In front of the stage there were big flowerpots. A movie theater car went around in the city with posters and music from the current movie. I only remember the Mickey Mouse movies that were just coming out then and that I loved tremendously.

6

Changing Schools

On the way to my elementary school, I regularly passed a horse cart that delivered milk. The nag whinnied from far away because it knew that I would give it the sandwiches my mother had given to me for recess. My mother wanted her moonlight princess to put on a little weight, and the slices of bread were buttered thick. I did not care for that, but I was happy when the horsy liked it. And my mother was very happy that I never brought anything back; she praised me for having eaten everything.

I do not remember any difference being made between Jewish and non-Jewish students before 1933, by my teachers or my classmates. I did not experience discrimination; my girlfriends were both Jewish and Christian. The only difference was that I had time off when the others went to religious education. I went once a week in the afternoon to the Jewish school. In the beginning our teacher was Dr. Stein, then we had Mr. Anschel, and in the end Mr. Blum. We studied the history of the Bible and learned to read Hebrew, but without understanding what we really read. My mother knew how to read Hebrew fluently, but she too no longer understood what she read. She had her Bat Mitzvah with Rabbi Dr. Jakob Winter, who even back then was not young anymore, but who was still holding office during my time. Winter, who had come to Dresden in 1886 as a young rabbi, died in 1940 at the age of eighty-three, and was thus spared the upcoming deportation. He had grown up in the Jewish tradition in Slovakia, and was known for his profound knowledge of Judaism and for his religiousness. He was also highly respected for his well-rounded general knowledge and education. At an advanced age he still recited odes from Horace in Latin. He was the quintessence of the rabbi who held a Ph.D., a development from the nineteenth century. My mother was very proud to have

My first day of school, 1930

studied with him, and saved the *Sidur* (prayer book) that she had received from him for her Bat Mitzvah. It was in dark red leather with
a golden lock and a dedication. This, too, was destroyed during the
bombing attack.

On the holidays, my mother and I went to the temple, as one called
the liberal synagogues in Germany at the time. The synagogue in Dresden was not just any ordinary building. We, the Jews from Dresden, referred proudly to the fact that it was designed by Gottfried Semper, the

Zeughausstrasse 1: Here was the residence of the Rabbi, the synagogue, and
the Community center of the Jewish Community

same architect who designed the opera house.[1] Built in the middle of
the nineteenth century, located on the central Zeughausplatz, it could
be seen from the banks of the Elbe River, and it belonged to the cityscape as much as the other more famous Semper building. The religious services were celebrated with an organ and a choir, which was
common at that time in liberal synagogues. For a time, I also went
to the religious service for children on Saturday mornings. We girls
sat in the gallery, and it would be an exaggeration to say that we distinguished ourselves by paying especially good attention. We had fun
throwing down little paper balls at the boys below us. For us there
would be no Bat Mitzvah.

When the Nazis came to power, I had just turned eight years old.
I do not have any memories of it. My parents avoided speaking about
political developments in front of me. They thought in any case that
the whole thing would not have a lasting hold on people's minds. One
year later, however, when my change from the elementary school to the
secondary school was in the offing, we could not avoid that topic any
longer. The city and the state secondary schools still accepted Jewish
pupils, but only in very limited numbers. Thus the choice of schools
was not easy. Ultimately, I was accepted at the Blasewitzer Secondary
Girls' School. Besides me, there were two other Jewish pupils in my
grade, Doris Feibusch and Ursula Friedmann.

In the classroom and in daily life the exclusionary measures started to become noticeable. I did well in gymnastics, but suddenly I was not allowed to take part in competitions anymore. I participated in two field trips in the beginning, but then I had to stay at home like my Jewish classmates. We were also prohibited from participating in swimming lessons. Essentially, we were not allowed to do many of the things that children did for fun. Moreover, they wanted to portray us as one imagined the Jews from the *Stürmer*: nonathletic, weak, and cowardly.[2] I imagine it was not easy for my parents to explain all this to a ten-year-old girl.

There were teachers who regretted this treatment, but most of the time they looked away like all the others who did not care. In the beginning some of them were especially nice to us. Soon this was not possible anymore. The nonsense began in the morning when the teacher entered the room. Everybody had to stand up and shout "Heil Hitler." We, the Jewish children, of course did not lift our arms and did not say anything. We did not perceive that as privilege but as exclusion.

In biology we had a teacher who was like a leader of the *Bund Deutscher Mädel*, a Hitler Youth group.[3] She was constantly drivelling on about the German race. She had her hair pinned up in a knot and wore a swastika on her blouse. She was certainly well suited to teach the new class about racial differences. However, she appeared to know the theory better than the practice, because at the outset she embarrassed herself terribly. When she came into the class for the first time, and was not clear about the composition of the class, she called me to the front of the class and declared loudly: "Here we have an example of an Aryan German girl." After all, I had blue eyes and long blond curls. I did not feel at all like laughing as opposed to my classmates, whom I saw grinning. But I had no other choice than to answer a bit shyly: "I am Jewish." From then on, she made life hell for me, because she could not forgive me. Our mathematics teacher was just as bad. He looked like one of Hitler's bodyguards: big and blond, and always in an SS uniform with the death's head insignia.[4] He bullied us three Jewish pupils and spoiled forever my appetite for mathematics. I could study as hard as possible, but bad grades were a certainty for me as well as for my two Jewish classmates.

Around 1938 we had to leave the secondary school—not because we were bad but simply for one reason: Jew. After all, Bernhard Rust, the Commissioner for the Prussian Ministry of Culture, had already announced in 1933 his desire to purify German schools "from all non-Germans . . . with all the brutality of duty."

Now only expensive private schools were allowed to take us. I was accepted in the Elisabeth School close to the Nürnberger Strasse; it was an all girls' school. It was really far away from home, and every morning I had to travel a long way on the tram. At fourteen, I just couldn't understand why things had to be this way. I was not allowed to see my previous school friends. When they saw me on the street they suddenly looked in another direction or crossed to the other side of the street. It was a terrible feeling when my best girlfriends simply ignored me. Probably their parents had hammered it into them. At that time, I no longer had contact with non-Jews. But it would get worse.

After a few months we also had to leave this school, because Rust, who was promoted to a Minister of the Reich, put into effect on November 15 a directive with the following words: "After the heinous murder in Paris, no German teacher . . . can be burdened with giving instructions to Jewish pupils. It also goes without saying that it is unbearable for German pupils to sit in a classroom with Jews."[5] Now there was only the Jewish preparatory school in the Fröbe Strasse, where all Jewish pupils had to go. There were some fine teachers there who had previously taught at other preparatory schools, for example my mathematics teacher Mr. Pinkowitz, and my German teacher Mr. Höxter. But they left the school little by little in order to emigrate, or they were deported like the Polish Jews in the October 1938 campaign.[6] I only have one picture left from my Jewish secondary school. It shows us with our English teacher Robert Kronenthal, nicknamed Bobby, whom we liked very much. He was married to a non-Jewish woman who could not protect him. One day he was arrested and we never saw him again, never heard anything from him again. They say that he had been listening to the BBC on his radio, which was strictly forbidden during the war. Apparently the neighbors had reported him and that was his death sentence. The fates of my classmates in the picture reflect well the few remaining alternatives at the time. My friend Steffi Cohn, who is in the picture, did not survive. She went to participate in the hakhshara, which provided training in farming techniques

Field trip to the countryside outside of Dresden, approximately 1939.
Our teacher Kronenthal (top row, center) and I (bottom right)

in preparation for emigration to Palestine, and asked me to come with
her. I did not want to leave my parents, nor did I want to go to Palestine. This hakhshara camp in Steckelsdorf next to Berlin was soon
closed, and the boys and girls did not go to Palestine but instead to
concentration camps.

In the picture you can see the siblings Kurt and Irmgard Nattowitz,
who were able to emigrate in time. The handsome fellow behind me
is Heinz Meyer; many of my girlfriends had a crush on him like I did.
He came from a musical family and he himself was an outstanding violinist, despite his youth. His brother Fritz played the piano. Both were

sent to the "Hellerberg camp" and deported to Auschwitz. Heinz survived amidst the most terrible circumstances. Among other things, he had to play violin with the prisoner orchestra at the ramp in Auschwitz. But I did not learn that until fifty years later, after he had already had an impressive career as a violinist in the Lassalle Quartet under the name Henry Meyer.

7
Excluded

Much had changed since the days of my early childhood. Despite my parents' attempts to placate me, when I was thirteen or fourteen years old, I felt that my childhood in effect was over. If I look back on these years, I remember most of all that I continually changed schools and homes. I especially hated that we had to move out of our apartment. I was deathly unhappy and cried. Moreover, my parents couldn't keep their movie theater. People tried to blackmail my father. Once he was summoned to the Reich's Ministry for Propaganda, where a Nazi suggested to him that he divorce his Jewish wife so that he would be able to keep everything. For him this was absolutely out of the question. Our family motto was to stick together, now more than ever. For my father this meant financial ruin. The one remaining photo of our movie theater is deeply symbolic. It shows the announcement of the 1930 premiere of the blockbuster film starring Willy Forst and the title—*The Song Is Over.*

It was a tragic irony that I would not be permitted to go to the same movie theater that had once belonged to my parents, because I was a Jew. After "Kristallnacht" on November 9, 1938, Jews were prohibited from visiting all cinemas, theaters, and other cultural events and exhibitions.[1] The sole exceptions were the performances put on by the Jewish Culture League—produced by Jews for an exclusively Jewish audience. Nonetheless, in the beginning, we sometimes dared to go to the movies. Since we didn't have the typical Jewish features we saw in antisemitic Nazi propaganda, we hoped we could remain unrecognizable. If an inspector would have come, this could naturally have turned out badly for us.

In the period immediately after 1933, there were still numerous inconsistencies between the Nazi laws and everyday reality. For example, I remember that for the Passover Feast, matza (unleavened bread) was delivered to the members of the Jewish community. A few non-Jewish schoolboys from the neighborhood gladly earned a couple of marks and rode their bikes to deliver to the Jewish families. As the door was opened, they stood at attention and greeted with a raised arm as they had learned in school: "Heil Hitler, Mr. Kohn, I've got the matza."

When my parents were forced to give up the cinema, it also meant that my paternal grandmother had to leave the home in which she had lived rent-free. She moved to Aunt Grete in Berlin, and from there she visited us often. Around Christmas of 1937, she pressured her daughter that she absolutely wanted to visit us in Dresden. Grete tried to deter her. The temperature was extremely cold then, and Grete feared she would catch a cold. But my grandmother was unstoppable; she insisted on visiting her son. My mother prepared a beautiful herring salad, we ate our evening meal, and my grandmother went to bed. During the night, there was suddenly a great commotion, and my father called out "Mother, Mother." I woke up and my mother calmed me: "Grandmother doesn't feel well, go back to sleep." The next morning I learned that she had suffered a heart attack and had died instantly. Dr. Ibner came over from the neighbor's house, but could only confirm her death. It was as if Grandma had sensed this and had wanted to see her son, her daughter-in-law, and her only granddaughter one more time. In retrospect, we often said that it was better that she didn't live to see all the horrible things that would happen to us.

The laundry woman hadn't been allowed to come to our house for quite some time; the careful and time-consuming preparations for the visits to the theater by my parents had turned for me into the past history of my childhood. The Café Pollender with its primarily Jewish guests didn't exist anymore for us. In our Central Park, Grosser Garten, we were still allowed to feed the squirrels, but the benches had signs stating "No Jews." The childhood of my former gentile classmates continued as usual, while mine was lost forever. Given the ever-increasing incidents of discrimination and exclusion, it became harder and harder to hold on to a piece of everyday life.

Starting in 1938 the restrictions grew rapidly. We were not allowed to enter certain parks, and more and more signs could be seen stating

"No Access for Jews." Every day a new prohibition was added. And then in August of 1938 we had to take a new name as well. We had to appear at the passport agency and received the additional name "Sara"; the men were given "Israel." Furthermore, they took our fingerprints, issued us so-called Jewish IDs, and stamped a big "J" onto them. We were registered like common criminals. And they made us pay for all of that as well.

In a sense, the song was definitely over in November of 1938. All the illusions we had held up until then were swept away with the "night of the broken glass." During the night of November 9, we heard loud noises in the apartment house where we lived as renters. People were trampling up and down the stairs. Someone said they were firemen. There must have been a fire somewhere, but where and what was unclear to me. We didn't know yet what was happening. Early the next morning, I went by tram to the Jewish school in the Fröbestrasse. Along the way my schoolmates and I always met up with each other. When those who lived in the city boarded the tram, they were incredibly upset, and when the tram passed by Zeughaus Platz, we could see from far away a large crowd and rising smoke. All of a sudden the word spread: "The synagogue is burning." It was impossible for us to go to school on that morning, since the Nazis were also raging there. They plundered Jewish shops, broke windows, and smeared graffiti everywhere: "Jews, get out!" The mob jumped at the goods. Jewish men were dragged from their apartments, and many were taken to Buchenwald.[2] For days Jewish citizens didn't venture out of their apartments. More and more often, the Gestapo came during the night, dragged Jews out of their beds, and deported them without any reason.

During these few hours, the Nazis had succeeded not only in destroying the center of a Jewish community rich in tradition, but also in stripping the city of one of its most impressive buildings. Of course we didn't encounter much sadness, let alone regret. If anything there were sneering reactions. The following morning we could read the official response in the Dresden newspaper, the *Dresdner Anzeiger*. Under the headline "The Jewish Temple is Burning," the report about the burning of the synagogue on November 10, 1938, read: "During the night from Wednesday to Thursday, around 2.10 a.m., the fire fighters were called to Zeughaus Platz. There they detected a fire had started in the

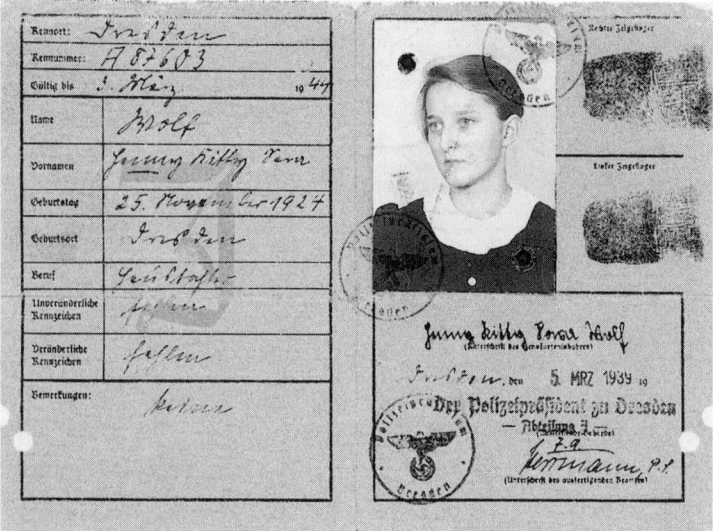

My "Jewish I.D."

synagogue, which grew rapidly among the dry wooden pews of the Jewish temple. Therefore, the firemen were unable to fight their way into the building. They had to limit themselves to protecting from the flames the adjacent residential buildings and the lumber yard next to the temple."

The truth was that the firemen came to extinguish the fire but were forced aside by SA members.[3] One courageous fireman, Mr. Neugebauer, succeeded in saving the Star of David that had been attached high on the dome. He hid it in his attic, thus placing himself in great danger. He returned it to the Jewish Community after the war.

That would have been the moment to leave. The Jewish School had just been closed. From here on, all formal school instruction was forbidden. The Jewish Community organized practical courses in painting, sewing, and photography to keep us busy, but also so that the children would have a trade if they were able to emigrate. And in fact, a few of my girlfriends went to England, while others went to participate in the hakhshara. That was not for me. Take a children's transport away from my family? No, there was never any question of that. And for my

The Dresden synagogue by Gottfried Semper

The destroyed synagogue after the pogrom of November 1938

parents, who meanwhile understood the necessity of emigration, there was no chance for a visa. So I took a painting and drawing class with Bruno Gimpel and a sewing class with Fanny Fanger. Actually, it had been my dream to study at the Art Academy in Dresden, and to design costumes for the opera. But it remained a dream that moved constantly farther from reality.

In our family, the thought of emigration had become an ever more frequent theme, even before "Kristallnacht." I was somewhere around thirteen years old when the first wave of arrests of Jews began. A few tried to escape arrest by having themselves admitted to the hospital, like my Uncle Max Rauch, who was on the Gestapo's list. Although no acute necessity existed, he had his appendix surgically removed and for the time being he was safe from the bloodhounds. Better an operation than to fall into the hands of the Nazi henchmen.

When he was discharged, a large family reunion took place in the Kaiserallee, admittedly not for joyful reasons. For the first time I met my Uncle Max and my cousin Esther from Copenhagen. They were there together with the Rauchs. Aunt Anna, my mother's older sister, had at this point already left Germany. Her daughter Paula had arranged for the rest of the family to emigrate to Bolivia, which they had reached after stays in Holland and Czechoslovakia. The situation for Jews in Germany was reaching crisis proportions. The Rauchs wanted to save some gold and other valuables and gave it to the Danes in the hope of having a little start-up money after they got out, something which unfortunately did not occur. The Danes, as we called them, wanted so much to take my cousin with them to Copenhagen. He had already been there frequently on vacation and could even read the Danish newspapers. I greatly admired him for that. But he could not bring himself to leave his parents. He would certainly have been able to survive with all the Danish Jews, who during one night in 1943 were brought to Sweden—that is, if he had not been on the one boat that sank on the trip to Sweden.

At thirteen, I didn't understand the significance of this visit and I remember only the pleasant parts. My mother cooked and set the table beautifully; the terrace to the garden was open and my cousin and I ran around happily. Above all, I remember the large tins which the Danes had brought me, filled with an enormous amount of licorice, maybe a half pound—licorice in every imaginable form: small little rolls, long rolls, square pieces, mostly black, but amongst them were always lime green and pale pink-colored little licorice pieces peeking out at me. As soon as they were out the door, I immediately shook the contents, which I found disgusting, into the garbage, but I liked playing with the big tins.

In 1940 I did not go with the children's transport to England or to hakhshara in Palestine. I did not go to Uncle Max in Copenhagen or to Aunt Anna in La Paz, but rather to Berlin, where there was a Jewish drawing school, which was run by ORT, a Jewish aid organization. Although my aunt Grete lived in Berlin, I could not live with her, because the government had commandeered some of her rooms, as happened with so many others during the war. My cousin Alfred was a dentist at the Jewish Hospital and found me a room at the home of one of his colleagues. I was living in Berlin and driving once a month back home to my parents. That wasn't at all pleasant; in Berlin I had to share a room with the daughter of the landlady, a Mrs. Cohn. The daughter, called "Pünktchen," was a nurse in the Jewish Hospital until she was deported. There were often air-raid alarms, and the first of my friends and relatives began to disappear. The circumstances around me became more dangerous from one day to the next. Once, I think it was in May 1941, I went as I did every morning to my school in Nürnberger Strasse. I found it closed. Overnight it had been shut down by the Gestapo. There was no advance warning, no word at all. So once again I would not be able to complete my career training. I packed my suitcase and drove back to Dresden. Despite the obviously deteriorating situation, I still believed what my father constantly repeated, probably also in order to pump up his own courage: "All this will not last that much longer." I heard him say this back at the beginning of the war, then during the attack on the Soviet Union, then during the battle of Stalingrad, and finally during the attack on Dresden as well. Yet even after that there was a seemingly interminable period of three months until our liberation.

8

With the Jewish Star in the Service of German Armament

In July 1941 I was assigned to a forced labor group in Dresden. I had to work in the Goehle factory of Zeiss-Ikon. We lived seven kilometers away from the factory, and in the beginning I was still allowed to take the tram, although not inside the train but standing outside on the platform. At Zeiss-Ikon there was a so-called Jewish section with approximately 300 people. Besides me, there were many other teenagers. They called us the "kindergarten," a term that I found much later in the diaries of Victor Klemperer. Klemperer wrote about us on May 3, 1942: "At Zeiss-Ikon there is a 'kindergarten' in the Jews' section. Jobs that have to be done with a magnifying glass by very young eyes. Girls of 15 and 16 work there. Protection of young people has been expressly annulled for Jews. Last week these children had to work day and night shifts so that they were working 24 hours out of 48; they are paid 27 pfennigs an hour."[1]

Our supervisor was a decent person for whom it did not matter that we were Jews. We did piecework and produced time detonators and clockwork mechanisms for submarines. This labor required strong concentration, dexterity, and good visual judgment. My eyes suffered greatly from this fine mechanical work, because we worked for hours every day without a break, under artificial light, with a magnifying glass and tweezers. At the same time as we, a shift of non-Jewish workers also arrived; we were not allowed to have contact with them, however. Already on the stairs there were bars to avoid any kind of contact. We called ourselves back then "people behind bars."

But even during these terrible years life went on for us. Like every

The Goehle factory, where I performed forced labor

girl at the age of sixteen or seventeen, I started to be interested in boys, and I started to turn some heads. There were the brothers Heinz and Walter Zonenstein. Heinz was the boyfriend of my friend Eva Wechselmann. His brother, like many Jewish men, especially the university graduates, had to lay train tracks. Word had it that the work there took extra long because one asked the other, "May I take the shovel, doctor so-and-so?" "Yes, please, professor so-and-so." Walter was perhaps eighteen years old at the time, with a pimply face, wet hands, and very shy. I was not interested in him at all, but he was after me. A common acquaintance told me later that he had given him tips on how he should get closer to me. Walter was too shy, however, and had probably never kissed a girl in his life. Unfortunately, he would also never have another opportunity to do so. Together with his brother, he was taken away on one of the first deportations. The father was stateless, and had already escaped to Belgium. The non-Jewish mother remained in Germany and was now alone.

We all knew very well that our survival opportunities differed radically depending on the combination of origin of our parents. Heinz and Walter were unprotected not only because "only" their mother was "Aryan," but because they themselves did not have a German passport. In fact, they did not have any passport: they were stateless. I, on the other hand, was lucky enough to have an "Aryan" father. And yet, I was disadvantaged compared to those of "mixed race" who had, to be sure, a Jewish mother, but who had been raised non-Jewish and therefore did not have to wear a star. My mother began with self-recriminations because it had been her wish to have me raised in the Jewish tradition. "Maybe it would have been better to do it the other way," she said, with a look at my girlfriends who did not have to wear the star. Every case in my circle of friends was different. The non-Jewish mother of one girlfriend, who had a Jewish father, had officially canceled the girl's membership in the Jewish Community after her father had escaped from Germany. That did not help the girl: she had to wear the star nonetheless and had to participate in forced labor with me.

For us, the decisive point during the Nazi period was September 19, 1941. As of that day, we were publicly branded: we were only allowed to go out on the street with the Jewish star. No Jew who lived in Germany at that time will likely forget what this meant. We couldn't believe it, even after all that had already happened. Everybody received this six-pointed yellow star that had to be sewn firmly on whatever piece of clothing you wore just then. If it was warm and you had it on your coat, you couldn't take off the coat. If it was cold and you had it on your dress, you couldn't put on your coat over it.

It was like running a gauntlet. At first my mother did not want to go out at all. It was horrible to venture out on the street with the star. Until then, we had been able to move around more or less incognito. Now, however, we were marked. Many people did not know, at least in the beginning, what kind of new law was in effect. They looked at me and asked what it all meant. The people in our street stared stupidly, even in our house they whispered because not everybody knew that we were Jews. Beginning in April, however, you could not only see that from our clothes but also on our apartment door, for there, too, we had to hang a Jewish star. We were to my knowledge the only family in Dresden where the head of the household wasn't Jewish but who nevertheless raised his child in the Jewish tradition, and hence had to hang a Jewish star on the door.

He who did not wear the star, or who hid it, was sent to a concentration camp or was murdered immediately. There were a lot of people who did not want to wear it or who at least tried not to. I know that based on what happened to a colleague from work. He went to work with the star, but held his briefcase over it. A black limousine drove past, the well-known Gestapo car, and he was dragged into it. He was never seen again. They did not even bring him to a concentration camp, they just killed him right away—for covering up the star. Some days later, they ordered his wife to the Gestapo headquarters and demanded, "What, you are not yet wearing mourning clothes?" She had thought her husband had only been arrested. Such were the methods of the Gestapo.

I never covered up the star. Just the opposite: I always wore it with pride. This also led to incidents of which I have various memories. Many people asked: "How does she end up with that, with her blond hair and blue eyes?" Things became particularly bad when we weren't allowed to take the tram anymore. In the beginning, they provided us a yellow painted tram, which brought the Jewish forced laborers from a central square to the Goehle factory. It left in the morning at five-thirty. At the same stop there were other workers waiting for their tram. Some were still very sleepy and wanted to get into our tram. Then the driver shouted, "Out, this is the Jew-train." They got upset about that: "What, the Jews even have their own train, and ours doesn't come." While we were getting into the train, they insulted and threatened us as if we had ordered our own tram. Once inside we heard such things as "Today they picked up this or that person," or "today the married couple so-and-so poisoned themselves with pills," or "they caught one as he was trying to get across the border." Every day we heard new reports of catastrophes on the way to work.

In March 1942 a new law was passed: Jews were not allowed to use the tram at all any more unless they lived more than seven kilometers away from where they worked. We lived exactly seven kilometers (4.4 miles) away and thus could not use the tram anymore. So I went with my bike to work. But I had an old rickety bike with poorly functioning brakes and worn-out tires. I was always glad when I arrived safely at my destination. Once, however, my tires became wedged in the tram tracks on the Carola Bridge.[2] I could not control the bike and I crashed. Stunned and dizzy, I lay on the street.

Next to me stood a young soldier, who helped me to get up. When he saw the Jewish star, he only shook his head. I realized that he was very sorry for what was happening to us. He advised me to bandage my knee. If someone had seen him helping me, it would not have gone well for him. The next day I stayed home sick. I did not like to do that, because whoever was sick for a longer period would end up in a concentration camp. Two days later, I repaired the bike and rode it again to the factory. I learned that this occurrence was by no means the rule when, a bit later, I had another accident with the bike and a young man helped me. This time I had exactly the opposite experience. He saw me bleeding next to my bike, helped me up in the beginning, but when he saw the star he let me fall like a hot potato and absconded as if confronted by a leper.

Then the Nazis ruled that all bikes belonging to Jews had to be turned in. Now I had to cover the seven-kilometer stretch by foot. The shift started at 6 o'clock a.m., so I had to get up at four and leave home at half past four. We had neither the proper clothes nor the proper shoes, and often we arrived totally soaked at the factory. Sometimes I had veritably frozen eyelashes after the seven-kilometer walk at five in the morning. But all of this was not so bad as long as it was dark. The way back was worse. It was daylight, and all who wore the star were afraid of that. Some people mobbed us or spit at us. Children often ran after me and shouted, "Jewish pig, Jewish pig! Get off the sidewalk!" I also came across people who said, "Keep your head up, you'll make it!" I assume that they themselves were involved in the resistance. There were not a lot of people who encouraged us, but there were also not a lot who mobbed us. Most of the people only looked away; they did not concern themselves with us at all. They were not as mean as the ones who mobbed us; they were simply cowards. Maybe they thought in silence, "Oh, how terrible." But they didn't have the courage to say it. They did not help us.

I always took the back way through smaller alleys. In one of those streets a young woman was always looking out of the window. I had gotten used to this when one day she was not at the window anymore but walking by me quickly in the street. I was afraid because that often did not bode well. Suddenly she put a piece of paper into my coat pocket without turning around or saying a word. We both kept on walking as if nothing had happened. When I turned the corner, I checked my pocket and discovered that she had given me food ration cards for sausage and meat. In the future, I always took another way to work in order not to bring the young woman into danger. There would have been bad consequences for us both if we had been caught. I remembered the girl's face, however, and looked for her after the end of the war. Her house was bombed out. I found her again by coincidence as the secretary of Dr. Friedrich, who was at that time the prime minister of Saxony.

We were also given food ration cards, but they were specially stamped. In red letters diagonally across the cards, stamped above most kinds of foods, was the word "Jew." There was a special machine for this. It was located in Leipzig and stamped only food ration cards for Jews in Saxony. No obstacle and no administrative challenge was too daunting for the Nazis. With the stamped food ration cards we only received very few kinds of food, such as dark flour. My father was the only one of us who received normal food ration cards, but they were not enough for all three of us. Sometimes he turned in all three cards together with his on top, and the baker or the butcher's wife, who knew of course that the other ones were stamped, cut off the stubs as if they were normal cards. Nobody, of course, was supposed to see that. It also sometimes happened that I gave the food ration card for dark flour to the baker's wife, and I discovered at home that behind the sales counter she had given me wonderful white flour and some rolls. These were all things that remained invisible to others. This constituted the assistance, or, if you will, the acts of resistance in everyday life that do not cost anybody anything and that were so important for us. Unfortunately, we experienced such solidarity only very rarely. I looked for the baker's wife after the war, by the way, but I could not find her since her shop was also bombed out.

My father could supply us with the essential things through acquaintances who had a large farm in the countryside, near the village of Graupa. He bought eggs and butter from them. Sometimes the bumpy bike ride via the suburbs of Hosterwitz and Pillnitz turned the eggs into scrambled eggs or the strawberries to marmalade. We really liked kernels of corn, which was in fact pig feed. My mother ground it and baked rolls with it. There was great joy when one day my father managed to acquire coffee beans. They were, however, still green, and first had to be roasted. We used a simple pot to do that. Then it smelled of coffee in the whole house, and our neighbors could have turned us in for that. But they were decent and left us alone. They did nothing good and nothing evil, they only left us in peace, something for which we were, to be sure, very thankful. Of course, my father could not make such purchases often, because it was war and hoarding carried the death penalty. If they had caught my father doing that, we would have been deported immediately. We knew that we only stayed alive if nothing happened to my father. And the Gestapo did everything to separate us. If the non-Jewish spouse died or got divorced, the Jewish partner or children were doomed. Beginning in 1940 the Gestapo interrogated my parents with ever-increasing frequency. The Gestapo men insulted and offended my father because he had married a Jewish girl even though, after all, there were enough "Aryans." They bullied my mother and accused her of fraud. They said that we had swindled someone out of the cinema we had owned before. She had to stand in a corner for two hours and let them spit on her. Some of the Nazis were notorious in the city. The man named Weser, he was the "spitter," and Clemens, he was the "beater." The worst thing was that you never knew ahead of time if you would get out again.

I, too, was once ordered to the Gestapo headquarters. That was in January 1945. I had received the order already before the Christmas holidays. The factory was closed and we wanted to spend the time relaxing at home. My father had received a goose from his friends in the countryside. I don't remember how this terrible letter got to me. I only remember that my mother fell apart and screamed: they are going to keep her there. My father grasped the goose and threw it onto the balcony, where it froze to stone. When the time came, my father accompanied me as we went by foot through the cold early in the morning, and he left me with the words "If you aren't out in half an hour, I'll come inside and wring their necks." Of course, we both knew that this was only a phrase. But he wanted to give us a little courage. The doorman shouted immediately at me: "SARA Wolf, that way up!" At first, I opened the wrong door—and was horrified. Inside the room was an iron bed, and I already imagined that they would keep me on such a rack over night. The interrogation as such was actually not as bad as the dread that preceded it. There were four or five men in the room, smoking cigars, in club armchairs. They asked about things that they already knew: if the marriage of my parents was a mixed marriage or not, why I wore the star, and similar questions. Everything was pure harassment. I will never forget when I came out of the building and I saw my father standing outside. He had aged years during the hour that I had spent with the Gestapo, convinced that they would keep me there.

We walked the long way back as fast as we could. My father, who unlike me was allowed to take the tram, got into it on the way back in order to return to my mother more rapidly. She was standing at the window, crying, and stared and stared. I can't describe the happiness we felt when we were united again. The first person who came was our friend Werner Lang, who had heard that I had been summoned to the Gestapo. I saw him cry twice: on that occasion and after he survived the bombing attack. Many Jews who received such a summons from the Gestapo preferred to commit suicide. But an inner voice had told me that they would let me go.

After they had tried in vain to convince my parents to divorce, the Nazis came up with something else diabolical: the non-Jewish husbands from mixed marriages would be drafted into the Organization Todt.[3] In this unit, which served on the front, you normally did not survive very long. The Jewish wives and children would then be defenseless and could be sent to a concentration camp. The Nazis could not totally abolish the law that privileged mixed marriages, and so they tried to finish their work in this fashion. My father, however, was protected from the OT by a well-known Dresden anti-Fascist, his old friend Dr. Fetcher. Dr. Fetcher had many Jewish friends, and my father visited him often in the evening in his medical practice. Once I accompanied my father on one of his visits to Dr. Fetcher and covered up my star on the street on the way. That was dangerous, but it would have been yet more dangerous if someone had seen a Jew visiting a non-Jewish doctor. He provided us with medicine, but more important, he gave us the courage to continue. During Dresden's capitulation to the Red Army, he walked toward the Russian tanks with a white flag and was ambushed and shot to death by an SS soldier. Today a street in Dresden bears his name.

We were always fearful when my father went away with the bike or the train, because there was always the possibility that something could happen to him. We were especially fearful because he not only helped us but also our relatives, whom he tried to provide with food. He went regularly, once or twice a month, to Berlin by train to bring the most essential nutrition to my cousin Alfred, whose dentist equipment was in our basement. Alfred lived there secretly in the apartment of a woman who hid him for money. He did not have any ration cards and he only could breathe fresh air when he opened the window at night. We supported him with the little we had. These visits brought my father into the greatest danger. Every time, we trembled wondering if he would return. Once he was almost caught in the train. He was sitting next to a man in a SA uniform when the eggs for Alfred broke in the bag in the overhead bin. The egg yolk dripped onto the SA man's uniform. He became terribly upset: "That is an impertinence! Who here still has eggs in wartime? That has to be punished!" My father acted alertly and behaved as if he knew nothing of the matter. He agreed with him: That was terrible, indeed. He also had no idea who could have left the bag in the compartment. In Berlin, he left the bag with the food in the train and arrived empty-handed at Alfred's. When he wanted to visit him again at the beginning of 1945 and nobody opened the door after he knocked, my father sat down in a restaurant on the other side of the street and observed the house. The restaurant owner, seeing that, came over to him and volunteered information in her Berlin dialect: "Well, they got the Jews this morning at five." If my father had come a bit earlier, they would have taken him as well. We never heard again from my cousin Alfred. He probably met the same fate as his parents in 1943, when they were deported to Auschwitz.

The deportations from Dresden to the East began in February 1942, when the first 500 Jews from Dresden were sent to Riga. The Jewish population grew smaller and smaller. The few "Full Jews" who still lived in Dresden had to go into so-called Jewish Houses. My aunt Paulina lived in a Jewish House in the Kurfürstenstrasse, so I often went to visit her. Horrible scenes took place there. Sunday mornings, when the Jews who had done hard work the entire week wanted to rest, they regularly had visits from the Nazi thugs Clemens and Weser. The two kept their fingers pressed on the doorbell buttons, pushed their way into the apartments, and terrorized the inhabitants. The "Spitter" spit in the pots with what little food the people had; the other slashed apart down comforters, pushed bread down the throats of old people, and made Jewish men recite prayers and dance to them. They entertained themselves with these "pranks." They also always took a few people with them, who would afterwards never be seen again.

The Jewish Community had to keep its people busy even on Sundays, according to the order of the superior authority, the Gestapo. They either had to shovel snow or do some other hard work. Dr. Neumark found something easier for me: he sent me to the Jewish House in the Lothringerweg in order to help an older woman there. Suddenly the doorbell rang in the familiar manner: long and never-ending. I knew what that meant, and I hid myself upstairs in a room, but I could, trembling, look into the hall through a crack. The "Spitter" and the "Beater" forced their way in, rummaged through everything, found an inkpot, and poured it over the beautiful white hair of the woman standing in the hall. Ink was not allowed for Jews. I was happy that, once again, I survived unscathed.

When the tide of war turned and the first defeats were reported, it became even worse for the Jews. As "Enemies within the Reich," we were made to feel every defeat. New laws to constrain us further were constantly introduced. We couldn't go to a hairdresser anymore. We were supposed to look like the figures in the *Stürmer*: unkempt and dirty. We did not do them this favor, however. The women braided their hair, or we found someone among our people who knew how to cut hair. We were only allowed to go shopping between 3 p.m. and 4 p.m. Even worse was the fact that we were not allowed to read newspapers. We also had to turn in our radio, typewriter, and telephone.

Wearing the star, we were completely isolated from public life. We were not allowed to enter certain parks, as well as the train station, libraries, museums, and restaurants. We could not stock food or buy flowers. Of course, we also were not paid appropriately. The so-called Jewish tax was deducted from our salary that was in any case miniscule.

From 1938 on, there was only one Jewish doctor available for all the Jews in Dresden, Dr. Katz, an elderly gentleman. Officially he was not allowed to call himself a doctor; he had a title similar to "nurse-practitioner." Katz was a German Jew who had fought in the First World War and who had been decorated with the Iron Cross. He was a German nationalist who could not comprehend why he of all people was being persecuted. He was always very proper, even a trifle cold I would say. Although I pleaded with him for a letter certifying that I was not able to walk many miles every day to and from work, he did not give it to me. He was also already a bit shaky. Once he gave me an injection and he must have hit a nerve; anyway, my arm swelled considerably, and I could continue working only with great difficulty.

I still remember well one story that was characteristic for the circumstances of that time, and which people told each other back then. A non-Jewish doctor lived near Dr. Katz. He took over all the former patients of Dr. Katz, who was only allowed to treat Jews. But that was not enough for him. He gave Dr. Katz a hard time whenever possible. One day an accident occurred on the street in front of Dr. Katz's house. Some people rang his doorbell and wanted him to come outside. At first he refused, because he was not allowed to treat non-Jews, but then his medical conscience triumphed. He went out on the street and who was lying there, run down by a car? The wife of that doctor. Dr. Katz gave her emergency care and her husband could not do anything about it. But if it had not been his wife, he certainly would have reported Dr. Katz, because he, as a Jew, had treated a non-Jew.

In November 1942, the "kindergarten" from Zeiss-Ikon was sent to a work assignment on the Hellerberg, at the city outskirts of Dresden. There, in barracks, stood wooden bunks. We had to stuff and stitch up straw pallets to put on them. It was obvious that a prison camp was being set up here, but we had no idea for whom. We thought it was perhaps for French prisoners of war. Not until some weeks later when

Dr. Willy Katz, the only physician allowed to treat us after 1938

all Jews, with the exception of those who lived in mixed marriages, were driven out of the Jewish Houses, did we realize that this camp was intended for our own people. Most of my colleagues were made to live in the camp as well, and they marched every day to Zeiss-Ikon, among them my aunt and my uncle, the Rauchs. They were all waiting there for their deportation. The Hellerberg was a kind of intermediate camp for the 300 Jews who were deported to Auschwitz in March 1943. When the camp was cleared again, only the Jews who lived in mixed marriages, and their children, remained in Dresden.

When I stuffed the straw pallets in Camp Hellerberg, I did not suspect that images from there would become visible to me again a

The Hellerberg Camp

half-century later. In the mid-nineties, I received a telephone call from
Dresden. Someone had discovered a documentary film about Camp
Hellerberg and the arrival of the prisoners who would be interned
there. A former laboratory assistant or photographer from the Goehle
factory had had to make a movie of it all for the factory directors.
When the Red Army arrived, the filmmaker appropriated the film.
Fifty years later, he gave the film to a well-known Dresden documentary filmmaker. After a good bit of painstaking work, he restored the
heavily damaged film to the point that it could be played again. But he
was not able to identify the people in the film. He invited me to Dresden so that I could view the film and contribute to the ongoing preparation of the commentary. I was terribly moved, for again I saw my
former girlfriends with whom I had worked at Zeiss-Ikon in the "kindergarten" and who had all been killed in Auschwitz.

9

Forced Labor in the Carton Factory

After the deportations of March 1943, our department at Zeiss-Ikon was closed down. It wasn't worth it to the Nazis to keep this workplace open for the few remaining Jews. Our destiny was uncertain, and we were terribly scared, because we didn't know what would happen to us. In March, however, there was certainty again; we were assigned new jobs. Some of us came to the cleaning company, Tempo, others to Mädler, a suitcase company, or to other small firms. From most of them you heard little good. People said that the boss of the carton factory was decent. This boss, Adolf Bauer, had requested twenty Jewish workers, and I went there as well. That was probably due to the intervention of Werner Lang, who in the past had often socialized with Bauer in Dresden's Sports Club.

The factory was located in a narrow lane. It was our job to produce ointment containers for pharmacies. I worked on cylinders where paperboards were agglutinated. On our work clothes we wore the yellow star and also a yellow belt, so that people could also recognize us from behind. Here too we did piecework, day and night shifts, always alternating. We were left in peace during our work, and we did not ask for more. I also did not have to walk as far as to the Goehle factory. All the same, my shift ended at 12 a.m., hardly a pleasant time for an eighteen-year-old girl to walk home alone for a few miles.

Once, still far away from our apartment, in the Borsbergstrasse, I heard footsteps behind me coming closer. A fellow who was obviously drunk was following me. He also tried to talk to me. I think he may have been a Croatian, of whom there were quite a few in Dresden at

The Gestapo was housed in this building

that time; in any case, he had such an accent. I ran as fast as I could and barely made it to our house door. He was right behind me, and stuck his foot into the slightly open door. Then I heard the voice of my father—and the drunk ran away. After that my Papa was so worried about me that he accompanied me for a while. But that was a lot worse, because now I also worried about him and beyond that it took twice as long. He didn't see particularly well in the dark, and I was constantly having to help him. Moreover, my mother was alone at home and we were worried about her. I said after a couple of days, no, I would prefer to go by myself, and it was, despite the unpleasant time of day, better like that.

One time when I had the night shift again, Mr. Bauer came in to us. He was in his mid-thirties, a tall, handsome man, always driving about with heavy motorcycles. In the beginning we were very mistrustful. He explained that he wanted to support us and that he was on our side. We had heard, however, that he was a National Socialist with a golden Nazi lapel button, and that he had already joined the SS as a young man. So we didn't know what to make of him. Sometimes he even brought us something to eat, although we told him not to do it, because we feared he could be discovered. He was, however, very naive in this respect, and he also greeted us on the street. Nobody was supposed to do that, least of all the boss, because we were practically his slave workers.

During the day, an "Aryan" shift also worked next to us from seven o'clock in the morning until five in the afternoon. We began at two o'clock in the afternoon and had no direct contact with that shift, but we stood for three hours next to each other. They noticed that sometimes Bauer had assigned us easy tasks. One night he came to us again, this time, however, with a different countenance. He asked us whether we hadn't kept our mouths shut, he told us he had had to go to the Gestapo. There they had told him that he treated us too leniently. He berated us, although we hadn't given anything away, of course; rather, it was due to his having acted so obviously. Now we were all scared: Bauer and us. That helped no one. After that we had to do heavy labor. First I worked with a labeling machine; then I had to work with a huge expander that punched heavy paperboards. The machine was so huge and heavy that it could not stand in the factory building, but instead stood in a wooden shed in the courtyard. We called it the witches' house. Terrible on-the-job accidents occurred there. One female prisoner of war accidentally got her hair caught in it and was scalped. Werner Lang was inattentive for one moment while feeding paperboard into a cutting machine, when I suddenly heard a scream and saw him covered with blood. He had instinctively put his finger into his mouth. After we had performed first aid, the only doctor permitted for us, Dr. Katz, came in a hurry and confirmed that Werner had cut off his fingertip. Werner was the type of person who had a joke ready, even in the most difficult situations. When he saw his severed fingertip, he declared that he wanted to insert it in spirits and keep it as a souvenir.

I also once had an on-the-job accident. I went down the old, caved-in wooden stairs into the workroom. I slipped on the recently cleaned wooden planks and landed with all my weight in a bucket filled with water. They had to be in every room, according to the bomb shelter rules—as if that would have helped during an attack. So I was sitting on the floor, my foot in the bucket, and the water gushing over my leg. I couldn't get up and everybody thought I had broken my leg. That was, fortunately, not the case, but my foot was stuck in the hole in the bucket. How can one perforate a bucket with one's foot? At that time, the buckets were made from thick paperboard. Werner Lang came running, a colleague came with a first aid kit, and I had to laugh loudly despite the pain. Now the nice bucket was ruined, Werner quipped. During my fall, I landed with one leg under a table that was behind the bucket. The table had a strip of wood on which I had cut open my leg. Werner Lang held the gaping wound together and another colleague applied a bandage. The worst part was, however, yet to come. I had to walk home and the next day walk to work again. The wound began to develop pus, and the bandage had to be changed. I began to tug on it very carefully; it hurt terribly. Werner Lang said, "Look out the window, look who's there." I did so and at that moment he ripped off the bandage with one motion. One can still see the scar today, and whenever the weather changes, it generally aches. There were not a lot of happy moments for us back then, but a half-funny and half-dangerous thing happened to me once. Bauer also produced antiseptic ointment containers for pharmacies. Once I had to carry a box with these antiseptic containers into another room. Right at that moment, Bauer entered with the Director of the Employment Office to whom he was showing the production of the ointment containers. As fortune would have it, the box opened at the bottom and all the tiny containers fell down onto the not very sterile floor. I froze in terror. Bauer pulled the director away quickly. And as chance would have it, his name was Beinlich, whereupon Werner Lang said to me, "Oh, how beinlich."[1]

My mother also had to do forced labor at Bauer's. Since she only worked during the day, we could not walk the long way together. My father, however, did not let my mother walk alone and accompanied her there and back.

One of my fellow workers for a short time at Bauer's was Victor Klemperer, who as we now know meticulously recorded these events in his diaries.[2] For us, he was a somewhat petrified old man, whose nationalist German attitude was known and not particularly popular. He was an example of what one calls an "absent-minded professor." It was not easy for him at work, and friends who lived with Klemperer in the Jewish House told us that he always took something to eat with him into the bomb shelter, but would forget his dentures in the apartment.

Eva Klemperer was a brave and courageous woman.[3] She not only refused to divorce her husband, she also helped many inhabitants of the Jewish Houses by taking care of little procurements. At the same time, she herself was in a difficult situation. She demonstrated the highest courage when she brought the diaries of her husband to the town of Pirna, not far from Dresden. That was mortally perilous—for her as well as for the doctor who hid them.

Such wives and husbands of Jewish partners, to whom my father also belonged, should be far more honored. There were also different cases. Women divorced their Jewish husbands out of fear of reprisals, and there were also men who did not want to compromise their career or their assets. In such cases, though, the Jewish partner was free game and could be deported immediately.

War prisoners, Russians and French, also worked at Bauer's. A Frenchman, Josef, often came to me to help me with the heaviest work. Huge paperboards, clotted with hot glue, had to be removed and inserted into rolls. "You rest half portion, I make you fast piecework." The Frenchmen got some chocolate in their rations, but would have preferred to trade it for bread. Josef sometimes laid a piece of chocolate, which we never got, near the window; I gave him a piece of bread for it. One of Josef's jobs was to deliver the completed ointment boxes to the pharmacies with a horse-drawn cart. One day, our doorbell rang at home. The horse-cart stood downstairs. Josef was sitting on it in his prisoner's uniform, with a red triangle tacked on the back. He had to deliver something in our vicinity and had dropped by to eat a bowl of warm soup. My mother gave him the soup, but she enjoined him never under any circumstances to come again. We would have been arrested immediately if they found out that a prisoner of war visited Jews. We too were not supposed to go anywhere without permission. That meant that the only public paths we could legally use were those leading to work, those for shopping (during the legally sanctioned times), and those to Dr. Katz, but only with a pass from the Jewish Community. After the war, somebody told us that during the bombing of Dresden Josef and his horse cart supposedly drove into a bomb crater of a destroyed bridge and plunged into the Elbe River.

Once we did not see Mr. Bauer at all for two weeks. Suddenly he entered with two men in long leather coats and slouch hats. I can still see him waiting at the door upstairs, deathly pale. He looked very shaken, with the two Nazis left and right of him. They picked out people and took them along. Among them was Mrs. Agunthe, whose husband had once been director of broadcasting at the Dresden radio station, and who had lost his position because of his Jewish wife. They said, "Where is the Jewess Agunthe?" The woman became as white as a sheet; she knew very well what was going on. "Come along!" was the order. She wanted to go to the toilet, in order to poison herself, we assumed. But they prevented her from doing that, and took her work clothes from her immediately. It was obvious that she would never return. We never heard from her again.

These selections went on, for days, for weeks. They came for us again and again. They always took someone. In 1944, Werner Lang was transferred from Bauer to the firm of Thinnig and Möbius. We assumed this was a punishment. Or did Bauer have to act under the pressure of the Gestapo? We had the feeling that Bauer and we had to suffer from his having treated us relatively well. We lived in constant fear of being the next ones they would come get. The fear was indescribable; it quite nearly drove us insane. We were exposed completely to the whims of the Nazis, because it was impossible to identify a system in their selections. Nobody knew whose number would be up the next day.

It was a terrible life. The fear was worse than everything else, worse than the hunger and worse even than the star. Mr. Bauer left us alone in the future; he did not do anything good, but neither did he do anything bad. In my opinion, he had hedged his bets. If things should change, if Hitler were finished, he could say he had behaved decently, and they would not harm him, even as a former National Socialist. I don't know if it really was like that; I at least believe it. He wanted some of us to remain alive so that we could testify for him. And, in fact, after the Nazi collapse, he demanded statements of support from us. My father, however, did not want to give him one because he believed that if Hitler had kept control, Bauer would certainly have handed us over to the Gestapo.

10

Only an Attack Can Save Us

One day in early 1945, Bauer told us that from now on there would be no more night shifts, just day shifts. We had no idea what that meant. On February 13, Werner Lang gave us a letter. He had the same job as Klemperer, working for the Jewish Council; both men were known as messengers of misfortune. The content of the letter was unambiguous: it was our turn now. We were told to assemble on February 16 at the Zeughausplatz square, where the synagogue had once stood, with travel provisions and blankets. We were apparently headed for a work assignment outside of Dresden. Lang himself, by the way, was selected for the deportation. According to his own journals, Klemperer was spared. Nobody knows why.

"Work assignment outside of Dresden" was a cover term for "concentration camp," most likely Theresienstadt.[1] We decided not to follow the order under any circumstances but to tear off the star and go into hiding. Even if this enterprise had little hope of success, it was definitely better than going to a concentration camp. If we must perish, then not in a concentration camp! Half jokingly, half seriously, my father said, "All that can save us is a massive attack on Dresden!"

We were not in the factory during the night from the 13th to the 14th of February. The only one there was the agent. In my opinion, Bauer and the high-ranking Nazi officials had gotten wind of the imminent attack. He wanted to save us so that we could testify for him after the war; at the same time, he wanted to get rid of his agent and a few others who knew too much about his Nazi past. And that is exactly what happened: the factory was in ruins, and the agent and his colleagues were buried beneath the debris. Had we been working the night shift as before, we would also have been buried beneath the rubble.

Many high-ranking Nazis fled to the countryside in the nick of
time, including Gauleiter Mutschmann, who managed first to save
everything in his villa, which he had, incidentally, stolen from a Jewish banker. He even rescued his carpets, but he neglected to warn the
inhabitants of Dresden. Naturally we didn't find all this out until years
later. We had not suspected an attack; nevertheless, we had clung to our
hope.

The sirens went off during the night of February 13, the night between Mardi Gras and Ash Wednesday. My father lay on the bed in
his street clothes; the deportation notice had paralyzed him. It was the
first time I had seen him on his bed in full clothing; otherwise he never
did that. First we thought the sirens were a false alarm, like the ones
we had often heard. The fact was, we no longer had a radio and had not
heard the report that entire flight squadrons were headed for Dresden.
Our doorbell rang. The air raid warden, an older, decent man, asked us
to come to the basement, although this was ordinarily forbidden to us.
My father replied: "But we aren't allowed to go down with you." "No,
come on down, all of you—come down to the basement with me," he
continued, and took us all down with him. We could already see the
"Christmas trees," triangular light signals above the sections of town
that were to be bombed. It looked ghastly. Not long after we went
down to the basement the firebombs rained down against our house.

Had we been in the factory that night, and had we gotten away
from there, we would have quickly ended up at the Jewish House in
the Sporergasse. It was an old insect-infested building bordered on one
side by the city wall. Friends that lived there always told us if there was
an attack we could hide with them, because the old wall would stand.
That is what happened in the end, but not as expected. During the attack, the impact of the bombs caused the house to collapse and buried
everyone in the basement. Nobody could rescue them despite the fact
that their knocking signals could be heard from the inside of the house
for hours afterward. There were no rescue workers in this inferno, let
alone tractors of the sort that could have broken down the old walls.
A physician, Werner Lang's brother, was among those trapped. We
hoped he had enough cyanide on him to spare everyone a grueling
death by suffocation. About 40 of the 170 Jews remaining in Dresden
died that day by the hand of their liberators, so close to the end. None-

theless, as macabre as it may sound, the attack meant our salvation. And that is exactly how we experienced it.

We were almost all women and children in the bomb shelter; the men were at war, at the front. We heard the firebombs above us—our house, too, had been hit. It was still standing, but it was burning. When we stepped out of the bomb shelter into the courtyard, the curtains of our burning apartment were blowing through the windows because the windowpanes were broken. My father insisted on returning to the apartment to fetch documents. I began to cry and tried to dissuade him: "Please, don't go!" I could not convince him. He returned at the last minute, just before the house was engulfed in flames. He had retrieved records about his former property on Alaunstrasse, along with a little money and some documents. Then we all began to make our way with masks and steel helmets to protect us against the smoke and falling stones. The first thing we did was tear the yellow stars from our coats. Of course we did not know exactly where we were headed; we just wanted to be in a part of town that was not destroyed.

We ran through burning Dresden, the Jewish stars and deportation orders stuffed into small rucksacks on our backs. We initially tried to be sure that the Gestapo headquarters was burning, and ran in the direction of the train station. We could not get through, but we inwardly rejoiced when people coming toward us reported that all the buildings behind the train station had been leveled to the ground. This would have meant that the Gestapo, along with all its records, had also burned down, or so we thought. Only later did we discover that some of the papers had been salvaged in time. Back then, however, the destruction of the Gestapo building offered some consolation.

Suddenly, around one in the morning, the air raid alarm went off again. Everyone ran, we as well, just to get to the next basement as fast as possible. Somebody was playing a radio, and we heard the second attack announced. Again, almost all of us in the basement were women and children. There was also a German shepherd, who had gone crazy and was howling loudly. My father immediately looked for the emergency exit, which was blocked off by sandbags. Being the only man, he tried to calm the women. About half an hour passed before we could get out. "We need air," I said. "Let's get out of the city; we have to run toward the Elbe River."

We ran toward the city. We had no way of knowing that the entire
city was destroyed and that everything was burning. Soon, however,
we realized that getting through the city would be impossible. A mael-
strom of fire surged out of a small alleyway behind the Altmarkt—the
Webergasse, I think—and threatened to suck us in. Suddenly, it looked
as though my mother would fly away. My father shouted, "Let's get out
of here at once." We got through to the Zeughausstrasse, where we
saw the Jewish Community Center in flames. Two days later we were
supposed to have met there to be deported to a concentration camp.
What irony that we now stood in front of that burning building with
the deportation order in our rucksacks! We looked for Werner Lang,
our friend, but in this building there was no longer anyone to be found.
Everywhere we saw notes written on house walls: "We're still alive.
We're at Aunt Ilse's," or something similar. Of course this was out of
the question for us; we knew we could not leave a trail. My father had
the idea of running to our house in the Alaunstrasse. But it was impossible to make our way there. Finally, we fled to the nearby meadows on
the banks of the Elbe.

Morning finally drew near. It was a cold day in February, and the
glistening red sun rose behind the black clouds. The sky remained jet
black for a long time. We kept running. Suddenly there was a roaring
sound above us: another attack. Along with the thousands that were
with us on the banks of the Elbe, we threw ourselves flat on the ground.
The bombs landed a few meters away from us. Slowly, it grew quiet,
and we stood up. Some remained on the ground, torn to shreds. Others
stood up but left an arm severed on the ground; others had a leg blown
off. It was a gruesome sight. The dead and injured were lying everywhere. Others had lost their minds; they sat naked, wrapped in blankets, murmuring to themselves. Corpses hung in the trees. My father
spoke to a child who lay next to us: "Come on, get up," but he could
no longer stand up. Suddenly my father yelled "Look over there—
the animals!" It was an incredible sight: animals had escaped from the
Sarrasani Circus and were roaming around on the other side of the
river. Weeks later, one heard stories about snakes from the circus ap-
pearing in people's basements.

We stumbled on. It must have been around noon when we reached
the Blaues Wunder, the Loschwitz bridge. A bomb had damaged it,

The ruins of Dresden

but it was passable. We knew a woman on the other side who had been
a forced laborer with me at Bauer's. She also lived in a so-called privileged mixed marriage—her husband was not Jewish. Everything was
still standing there. The districts of Loschwitz and Weisser Hirsch had
not been bombed. We were so covered in soot that she did not recognize us at first. We were able to stay with her a couple of days, sleep-
ing in camp beds. She brought us some potatoes that we ate with the
peelings, to my Mama's dismay. Werner Lang came after a few hours.
We had previously been searching for him and discovered that we had
passed each other amidst the chaos. Each thought the other had been
buried beneath the bombs.

II

Waiting for the End

After a few days the doorbell rang. And who stood in front of the door with a heavy motorcycle next to him? Mr. Bauer, whose house had been bombed out. We were no longer afraid of him at this point, but he feared us. Initially we had thought everything would fall apart after the attack; it would not only be the end of Dresden but also of the Third Reich. There was simply no other way to understand this inferno. It seemed impossible that life would continue as normal in the aftermath. But sadly, the end was not as near as we had hoped. Time would reveal those last months of the "Thousand-Year Reich" to be the most agonizing for us.

Our acquaintance had somewhat befriended Mr. Bauer and took him in, as the two had started making plans earlier. Had it come to the point that she were to face deportation, she was to disguise herself as a Red Cross nurse and help in a military hospital. He would have supplied the uniform. In case of an attack, she had promised to give him shelter, provided her house would still be standing. When Bauer then remarked something to the effect of "Surely you don't intend to turn your house into a Jewish stronghold," she advised us to leave. She could not accommodate so many people in the long run. We understood that our presence jeopardized her and her husband. But we had nowhere to go or stay. We took our handcart and trekked through the bombed city. After the attack it was common practice simply to move into empty houses just to have a roof over one's head. Along with Werner Lang, we went to a house in the district of Blasewitz that had also belonged to a "mixed race" couple. The couple had fled to the outskirts of the city. We were no longer registered, and we wanted the authorities to assume we were dead. We never left the house at daytime until May 8.

Only my father went out now and again to get food, because he still had food stamps. He rode an old bicycle to the countryside in search of something to eat. These ventures were anything but safe. First of all, timed detonation bombs were still exploding. Second, several smaller air raids followed the first big attacks. And, third, hoarding was punishable by death.

My father was able to obtain bicycles for my mother and me, because we were constantly thinking of escape. Escape from the Germans, escape from the Russians.... The best hideaway may have been in the country. Who knew just how useful a bicycle might be, my father reasoned. Unfortunately, all his efforts came to naught. Our attempt to flee to the country failed due to my mother's lack of skills when it came to riding a bicycle. Werner, who lived in the same house, went to great pains to instruct her in the art of cycling. Of course, he did this in the dark and in the back yard, as we could not leave the house during daylight. She just kept leaning against him instead of sitting straight. I heard him calling desperately, "It does help if you pedal!" She was hanging across the handlebars crookedly while he tried to run and push the bike at the same time. He even tried moving her feet up and down. By no means did we feel like laughing during that time, but I could no longer control myself and burst into loud laughter. All efforts had been in vain; we stayed in the city. Werner sighed heavily: "All that for nothing."

One day there was a turbulent ringing of the doorbell. We were frightened by the slightest noise, especially the ringing of the doorbell, because we always thought they were coming for us. It was not the Gestapo, however. Instead, it was Ernst Neumark, a Jewish attorney. During the Nazi era he was only allowed to call himself a "consultant." An honest and upright man who could never have done anything wrong, he walked about still wearing the Jewish star. He was a "Liaison of the Reich's Coalition of Jews in Germany." He jeopardized his own safety and that of others by the way he acted—the Gestapo had spotted him walking in the street not long after the attack. The infamous black limousine had stopped, and he was yanked inside and interrogated: "What, you're still alive, you Jewish pig? By tomorrow we want all the addresses of the surviving Jews in Dresden." In his despair, Neumark turned to us and reported the incident, which in turn was dangerous for us, since somebody could have followed him. He then fled to the woods. He never actively betrayed anyone. Nevertheless, we were shocked to discover that after the attack and utter chaos, the Gestapo had nothing better to do than search for the surviving Jews in Dresden. We felt how long a quarter year could last.

The worst was yet to come. One day we looked out of our window and saw a family with children headed straight for our house. The man wore an SA uniform and had a wife and two children. They looked determined, and were dragging a handcart behind them. They moved into our house; only a wall separated us. We feared the man knew our real identity; it was obvious that we never left the house. Once when the SA officer was listening to the radio, Werner was eavesdropping at the door. At that moment, the door opened. Luckily, however, nothing happened. The children were horrible. They were always screaming: "The Führer still has a wonder weapon," and "When the Russians come, we'll pour boiling water on their heads." When the Russians actually came, everything was completely different. We came close to turning them over to the Russians, but my father prevented it. He felt it would not have been right to deprive the children of their father. On May 7, when we could hear the Russians' tanks approaching, the SA officer burned his uniform and his children laid their swastikas on the tram tracks. They wanted to erase every last trace. The SA officer himself was stone drunk. He babbled that he had a Jewish grandmother in America—out of fear and to save himself. So he knew that we were Jews.

12

Liberated—and Still Full of Fear

On May 8, the Russians came—our liberators. The tanks rolled over
the Blaues Wunder bridge with their troops. The first thing we saw
were the soldiers who forced their way into houses in order to plunder
and to rape the women. In the beginning we were actually glad. At that
moment, after all the years of humiliation and fear, we simply thought:
they deserve it. But we soon realized that we also needed to be on our
guard and that we were the victims again. Nothing interested them
besides madka[1] and vodka. We called out to them: "Evrej" (Jew), but
they just laughed and answered: "Nix Jew, Hitler all kaput, you spy!"
So we fled to the basement with the Germans. There my father found
a hiding place for the women. There was also a small child with us
whose mouth we had to hold shut so that the Russians would not find
us. We would never have dreamed that we would initially have to hide
from our own liberators. The soldiers tapped against the walls with
their guns. My father then led them through the house. When they
neared the basement, he intentionally dropped the lantern. We heard
a shot and thought, "Now everything is over. We survived everything,
but our liberators have killed my father on our first day in liberty." The
Russians felt nervous in the dark and I heard how they left the house.
I climbed outside through the basement window and spotted my father. He, too, had been able to find safety by climbing through a basement window.

We thought these scenes might repeat themselves every night, so we
fled from that house into the ruin where we had been bombed. There
the situation was even more frightening and unpleasant. Finally we

heard about an apartment belonging to some friends of ours that was still halfway intact. That's where we moved. The next night however, the same commotion started all over again. Gun butts were slammed against the door amidst a confusion of voices. I tried again to convince the Russians that we were Jews who had survived here in hiding and was met, like the night before, by unbelieving stares. This time, however, I began by reciting the "Shema Yisrael" prayer and by showing them my yellow star. Among them was a Jewish officer. He stopped the other soldiers, who immediately left us in peace. Gradually, during the next few weeks, the situation calmed down. A military headquarters was set up where we received our identity cards, written in German and Russian, as Victims of Fascism.

It was mid-May, hot and humid. When we walked along the streets that had been bombed, the intense smell of corpses was still present. I wanted to leave the Emser Allee, because there the threat from the Russians was the greatest. So we took our cart and, along with Werner Lang who pulled it, made our way toward Borsbergstrasse, where friends of Werner lived who were refugees. We were able to stay with them for about fourteen days, until we were assigned an apartment. Our identity cards now also protected us from the Russian soldiers. That is, they were meant to protect us. They did not always help. Once some Russians pulled my father off his bike and stole his watch. He protested, showed his card, but they just laughed: "Card yours, watch mine."

The first thing we wanted to do was to find our relatives again. Hence we contacted our family members in Denmark and Bolivia. It took ages for mail to be shipped back and forth. Our relatives were overjoyed upon discovering that we were still alive. Only after the war did we find out that all Danish Jews, among them my relatives, had fled to Sweden and thus were saved. We turned to refugee search organizations to trace our remaining family members. We especially thought my cousin Alfred would still be alive. After all, my father had secretly brought him food just a few months before. We hoped he had been able to hide elsewhere or had escaped in the chaos of the past months after the Gestapo had arrested all the other Jews in the house in January of 1945. My father thought we needed to search for him in Berlin, but getting there seemed impossible at the time. Trains were not running yet. In this situation, too, Werner Lang again came to our aid. He was able to arrange for a car, which we drove to Berlin to find Alfred. Berlin resembled Dresden: a single heap of ruins. We were unable to find the woman who had hidden Alfred. We visited Aunt Grete, whose home had not been bombed and who was sharing it with one of her female friends. She died in 1947 during the great typhoid pandemic in Berlin. But there were no signs of life from Alfred.

Some acquaintances from Dresden, only a few, returned from concentration camps, and only then did we really begin to comprehend the scope of what had happened. To be sure, we had known during the war that death camps existed; we had often heard the name "Auschwitz." And after receiving the deportation order we were determined to do everything but obey it. My father had said at the time, "I'd rather have a bomb fall on my head than go to Auschwitz." We didn't know that Auschwitz had already been liberated by then. Nor did we know that people were being gassed to death in industrial fashion—that went beyond anything we could imagine.

Despite all these horrors, the details of which became clearer every day, we never considered leaving Dresden or Germany. My father was convinced he would now be given a movie theater again. He thought the Russians would have to make exceptions for those who had been persecuted. Surely it was not possible to withhold property from its rightful owners after it had been stolen by the Nazis. He now began a battle with the public authorities, and his war with them lasted seven years. We were told to pay property tax on the land that still belonged to us, but on which a house stood that was uninhabitable—a bombed house. He requested he be given another cinema to manage. It had belonged to Nazis, but he was unsuccessful anyway. We needed something from which to live. Returning to the banking business was hardly an option under the Communist regime. The rulers of neither the Soviet occupation zone nor of East Germany pursued a policy of reparations payments to Jews. The authorities did not care that we had been persecuted. They distinguished between two separate groups. On the one hand were the "victims of fascism" who had "only" been persecuted, like us; on the other hand were the "fighters against fascism," who were basically Communists during the Nazi era. If they didn't also happen to have been Communists, Jews were more or less second-class victims. An example of this is the case of the head of the Leipzig Jewish Community, Eugen Gollomb, who after escaping from Auschwitz joined Polish partisans fighting the Nazis. Despite his actions, he was denied the status of a "fighter against fascism" on the grounds that his insufficiently developed "class consciousness" suggested the absence of "conscious political motivation." We sensed this especially at the headquarters of the VVN, (the Association of Those Persecuted by the Nazi Regime)[2] founded in 1947. My parents received a small pension; I got nothing, not even the possibility of an education. There were differences even when it came to food rations. We were given less than the "fighters against fascism." But my father said, "We survived the Nazis; all this won't bother us too much."

Of course, we could have easily changed everything by joining the Communist Party. There were a few who did this by conviction, but naturally there were also those who had been very bourgeois before and now immediately joined the Communist Party, the KPD, such as Victor Klemperer. Others were automatically registered with the new Communist-Socialist Unity Party (SED)[3] without their assent, simply because they had been registered as Social Democrats earlier. My father was terribly upset about those who now suddenly strived to enter the Party or somehow identified themselves with the symbols of the new government. On the first of May and other occasions, for example, we were to hang flags with the hammer and sickle from our windows. My father merely commented, "I never waved any flags during the Nazi period, and I'm not about to do it now." I was unable to attain admission to a college or university because I belonged to the bourgeoisie; I was neither a farmer's nor a worker's child, and I refused to join the SED. The fact that the Nazis had forced me to discontinue my school education was of no interest to anyone. I should very much have liked to attend the art academy, but that goal was unreachable.

Despite all the disappointments, however, we were happy that all three of us had survived the years of war and persecution unscathed. A whole family—that was a rarity! We relished the fact that we were allowed to walk the streets like normal people, without being marked; that we could enjoy parks; that we did not have to shudder each time the doorbell rang fearing it could be the Gestapo. We prized sitting on a park bench that had formerly read "No Jews Allowed." I was allowed into a movie theater, a theater, a restaurant, again.

УДОСТОВЕРЕНИЕ	**Ausweis**
Предявитель сего Хенни В о л ь ф	Herr Henny W o l f
25.II.1924 Дрезден рожд. в	Frau geb. am 25.11.1924 Dresden
Д р е з д е н A 36 прож.	wohnhaft D r e s d e n A 36
Винтербергштр. 86 c	Winterbergstr.86 c
является членом Еврейской общины г. Дрездена.	ist Angehörige[r] der Jüdischen Gemeinde zu Dresden

Dresden, am __24.1._____ 194 7

Der Vorstand der
Jüdischen Gemeinde zu Dresden

My I.D. in Russian and German

Of course, compared to the time before 1933, life was far from being back to normal. The opera and the theater houses had been destroyed. At first, they held theater performances in temporary facilities behind the spa in Bühlau (we nicknamed the building "the barn"). We sat freezing on wooden benches, but the quality of the shows was outstanding. The theater was in any case a new experience for me. I could only recall the children's theater from the time when I had still been allowed to go out. Things were, however, quite different from the elaborate preparations my parents had made for visits to the theater in years past. Nowadays, we had no seamstress to make us custom-tailored clothes; we were glad to have clothes on our backs at all.

When going out to eat and ordering a potato dish, one had to give the cook half a pound of potatoes in a small sack—per person. So whenever we went out, we carried a sack of potatoes with us. Food stamps were sufficient for ordering meat. All restaurants belonged to the State Trade Organization. For us, this was nevertheless like paradise; we had almost forgotten what the inside of a restaurant looked like.

My parents received a pension, but it was not adequate for black market prices. My father consequently obtained a trade license and opened up a small store with textile goods. Unfortunately, there were hardly any goods for him to buy. The manager of a hat factory in the district of Niedersedlitz, who had himself been politically persecuted during the Nazi era, always gave my father a little more than he would have been entitled to according to State rules. Once the delivery contained boxes filled with dark gray, felt-like ski hats with ear warmers: terribly ugly, but warm. The men stood in line two hours before the store opened that morning. Word had gotten out that warm ski hats were available. They literally tore them from our hands. We did not make a large amount of money with them, but had something that could be exchanged for butter or eggs in the country. There everyone was still by and large using a barter system. A few eggs in return for a shawl for the farmer's wife, some poultry for a piece of cloth, or, as Werner Lang jokingly put it, "I'll trade you a well-preserved skeleton for a pound of goose fat."

Thanks to my father, then, we were not suffering from hunger like so many others around us. Additionally, we had clothing and did not have to freeze. But for my father, who was in his mid-sixties, it was not easy building a new existence. He saw his store mainly as a temporary solution and never stopped dreaming of his movie theater. My mother and I helped him in his store. For my mother this situation was naturally very unusual. She had grown up in a world in which women did not have to go to work. To be sure, the Nazis had made her perform forced labor during the war, but if it was not necessary, a woman simply did not work. My father incidentally had the same ideas and felt uncomfortable having to depend on my mother's help.

I tried to make up a little for my lost social life and often traveled with friends; I spent summers in Usedom[4] and went skiing in Oberbärenburg[5] in the winters. In Dresden itself the Jewish Community that had just been reestablished became the center for all my social activities. Prayer was initially held in the meeting rooms on Bautzener Strasse. My mother regularly attended services there with me. For Jewish holidays such as Purim[6] and Hanukkah, the congregation rented a room where we held banquets with music and dancing. My mother, along with other women, baked Haman's pockets ("homentashn"), the traditional triangular Purim pastries. We were connected to the Community and we were happy that there was Jewish life again, that there was at least an appearance of normality. Most members of the Com-

The Synagogue in Fiedlerstrasse, dedicated in 1950

munity were not originally from Dresden, but were Eastern European Jews who after their liberation had remained in Germany as "Displaced Persons." In 1947 there was a total of only 135 members. Some of those were not from Dresden at all, but from surrounding areas. There was almost no one my age. Of the former inhabitants of Dresden, most members had lived in mixed marriages; many would not have identified themselves as Jews before the Nazi era. Now they were searching for some form of security in the Jewish Community. In 1950, a new synagogue was dedicated. One could not have imagined a greater contrast than that between the imposing, confident, and widely visible form of the former Semper Synagogue and the humble building on the property of the Jewish cemetery on Fiedler Strasse. Although the synagogue was again teeming with life, the building was nevertheless reminiscent of a morgue on the grounds of the cemetery. What could have been more symbolic for the existence of Jewish life in those years?

13

The New Threat

New persecutions by the Communists soon overshadowed the seemingly quiet postwar era. Our friend Werner Lang, who temporarily worked as State Secretary for the Regional Government in Saxony, then as Director of Saxony's Engineering Department, suddenly disappeared one day. The Secret Police picked him up at his office—for no reason. The same thing happened to many other Jews in important positions.

I was beside myself when his secretary appeared at the front door of my apartment in tears and reported what had happened. I was convinced there had been a mix-up and that he would return the next day. He was a real textbook "yeke," very meticulous, never capable of the least transgression. With the help of a lawyer, I tried to get a message to him in jail—without success. Together with my parents we desperately searched for a way to bail him out. I finally thought of Ruth Glücksmann with whom my mother and I had worked at Zeiss-Ikon and who was now married to Jule (actually Julius) Meyer, the cochairman of the still united Jewish Community in Berlin. Jule Meyer was also a Representative in the National Parliament, the *Volkskammer*. If anybody could help, he was the one. I had met Ruth again after many years when the synagogue in Dresden was dedicated in 1950. She had invited me to come to Berlin sometime, and told me of the interesting events held by the Jewish Community there. I now accepted that invitation—I think it was during a Purim celebration. My reasons, however, were not social ones. I sought the connection to help out Werner Lang, because Jule Meyer, so they said, had helped get several people out of jail.

I could not mention my real intent when I spoke with Ruth over the phone. So I simply informed her that I was accepting her invitation. Soon I visited her in her lovely villa in Klein-Machnow, outside Berlin. Everything was very elegant, with a chauffer, a housekeeper, and a maid. The meals were wonderful. This was a different life from what I had seen thus far in East Germany; this was how the officials lived. For this couple, though, I was glad; they deserved it having gone through so much and having survived Auschwitz. I must have looked pretty terrible, and Ruth soon asked what was wrong with me. I merely said, "They've arrested the doctor." She flung her hands into the air exclaiming in horror, "It's starting again!" They knew that Leon Löwenkopf, chairman of the Dresden Jewish Community, and others had also already been arrested. She threw her arms around her husband: "Jule, Jule, you have to help. They've arrested Werner." He did not even respond. He could hardly admit in front of me that he was able to help. I rode back to Dresden. The same scenario repeated itself: there was no way to get to the prison or to establish contact in any way. For a time I felt as though I was being followed, though I cannot say for sure this was the case. I returned to Berlin several more times to speak with Jule Meyer and his wife. In December, after nine months, Werner Lang was suddenly released. I never found out if this was due to the Meyers' efforts.

14

Everything Is Lost Again

We now felt increasingly unsettled. The number of Jews in leadership positions who were being arrested grew steadily. When the authorities found Hebrew texts, be they mere prayer books, they immediately grew suspicious. Jews were quickly accused of having Zionist-imperialist contacts. The peak of this hardly veiled antisemitic campaign was a show trial against the "antigovernmental conspiracy" centered around Rudolf Slansky in Czechoslovakia during November 1952.[1] The majority of the accused were Jews; the antisemitic hysteria, disguised as anti-Zionism, was unmistakable. As we know today, a similar show trial was prepared for East Germany.[2]

It was the height of the Cold War, and the leaders of the Jewish Communities in East Germany had to express their solidarity with the Soviet Union on every occasion. Once I went to one of the speeches by Jule Meyer. His wife was sitting next to me, and when he fulminated against the capitalist enemies, she took hold of my hand and whispered in my ear: "You will see, this won't end well." In fact, besides Leon Löwenkopf, other prominent Jews in East Germany were arrested, such as the journalist Bruno Goldammer and the chairman of the National Front in Saxony, Hans Schrecker.

We grew frightened again, simply frightened. We did not want to repeat all that we had been through. During my last visit to Berlin I had also been warned by Heinz Galinski that something was in the works, and that our safety in East Germany could no longer be assured.[3] "Why are you still there?" he demanded. I wanted to know in return: "What should we do in the West if we suddenly show up there?" He assured us that the Jewish Community would certainly help us. His wife, Ruth, by the way, was originally also from Dresden. The

Jewish Community in Berlin was at that time practically the only in-
stitution that was still united in East and West, but a division already
manifested itself; then in January 1953 the split took place. The city
of Berlin was still not separated by the Wall; one could ride with the
light rail *S-Bahn* to West Berlin, though of course one needed to go
without luggage in order to avoid attracting attention. That meant that
we would have to give up the little bit of home that we had established
in Dresden after the liberation. But it was I who in the end pushed for
giving up everything and leaving East Germany. My father had also
grasped in the meantime that he wouldn't get his movie theater back.
After we had made our decision, my mother and I went three or four
times to West Berlin in order to take some clothes and the most essential things over there. Furthermore, we tried to carry some goods
from my father's business to the West, because we would have to live
on something in the beginning. We did not want to depend on our acquaintances, and my mother was ready for everything except a refugee
camp. It was never possible to take more than a few things, and every
passage was connected with risks. We left the things with an old friend
of my father's.

One day when I was taking the train to Berlin with my mother, the
East German police asked for our papers. Once again, the identification card of my mother attracted the attention of the officials: birth-
place Minsk, first name Sascha. The policemen looked very suspi-
ciously at the passport and asked where we were planning to go. We
had the identification card from the Jewish Community with us and
claimed that we would visit the Community in East Berlin. Naturally
nobody says in such interrogations that he or she wants to go to West
Berlin. One of the policemen looked at the luggage and asked what
we wanted to do with it. We answered we would stay a few days, and
therefore we would need the luggage. Unfortunately, the same police-
man showed up on the return trip. We were almost paralyzed with
fear when he stepped into our compartment, because we were now of
course without luggage, which should have immediately raised suspi-
cions. Fortunately, he did not remember us, and passed by. Another
time my father accompanied me. We were taking chiffon cloth from
our shop with us in order to be able to obtain some hard currency in the
West after our escape. I filled my suit, my pantyhose, and bra with the

chiffon cloths, which did not attract attention. This turned out well. It was more difficult when we once tried to check in a suitcase with bras and corsets of all sizes at the train station. We carted the suitcase to the train station of the Neustadt district, but our suitcase was no longer the newest, and on a busy square, the Postplatz, it burst. Bras in all sizes and variations were lying in the dirty November snow and attracted the attention of the women standing there. "Can we buy this? Can we have this?" They jumped at it, and we tried to escape as fast as possible. My father locked the suitcase in a makeshift fashion and checked it in at the train station. If it arrives, that's fine, if it does not arrive, the goods are simply missing. The suitcase did arrive and helped us in the beginning to build a modest start-up fund.

On December 6, 1952, we were finally ready. The date for our escape was connected with a Hanukkah ball in East Berlin. We had an invitation for the ball, a good excuse at the controls between Dresden and Berlin. There were no big farewell scenes, because we didn't want anyone to know in advance of our plans for escape. It would only have brought us as well as others into unnecessary danger. Only very few people knew of our plans—for example the friends with whom we pleaded to take a painting that was very dear to us; for them it seemed too dangerous. They only took the rest of our food. The friend who finally took the painting escaped a bit later to the West herself.

My mother thought she absolutely needed to take down comforters with her. We had acquired them with considerable effort. She did not want to sleep in "horse-blankets" in the event we would have been placed in a refugee camp. She wrapped them into long rolls, covered them with packing paper and fastened them together. Furthermore, at the last minute, she packed our silver cutlery in a small black bag. Without saying a word about this to my father or to me, she put sandwiches on the top of the silver. We were convinced that the bag only contained victuals for the voyage. The long, rolled-up comforters, of course, attracted the immediate attention of the police officer, who asked us in his Saxon dialect what we had lying there. My mother told him unblushingly that we were invited to the Jewish Community in East Berlin for a few days and that we had to bring our own comforters. To our collective astonishment he believed this story and did not check the bogus travel bag.

With all these things we got into the *S-Bahn* train: then we realized that we were being followed. A man, whom we already had noticed in the train from Dresden, now breathed down our necks in the *S-Bahn*. We heard an announcement: last station in the East. We had planned on simply riding nonstop to the West, but we were attracting a lot of attention with our luggage. Our shadow surely would have arrested us before the train moved on. So we exited the train, and our shadow was right behind us. He was only waiting for us to board the next *S-Bahn* toward the West. My father was alert enough to go out of the train station and to call a taxi. He shouted to the driver: "Just get out of here as fast as possible!" The taxi driver knew immediately what was going on and answered in his Berlin dialect: "I can't drive you to the West." "No, no, drive us to the Oranienburger Strasse, to the Jewish Community!" We lost the man shadowing us. The Jewish Community was an unscheduled stop, but it proved the right move. Jule Meyer unlocked a storeroom for us where we could leave our belongings. We boarded the *S-Bahn* without the luggage and went to West Berlin. My mother had to get along without her comforters, but she never let the sterling cutlery out of her hands. Fortunately, we had already stored some clothes with the acquaintances with whom we first stayed. A friend brought us the down comforters from the East to the West after a few weeks.

After a couple of weeks in the Berlin Tempelhof district, where we stayed with my father's old friend, we finally got a room for the three of us. I had to sleep with my mother in one bed; that was okay because both of us were very thin and there wasn't space for a third bed. The landlady did not want to give us the room at first; one room for three people! Her German shepherd, however, saved us. When my father and I went to look at the room, the dog leapt toward us. I like dogs a lot and said immediately, "Hey Cutie, come here." The landlady was astonished that her pet jumped toward me and wanted to play with me. She told us in her Berlin dialect, "Well, you know, if he likes you that much, you get the apartment. Normally, he doesn't like strangers."

Despite that, we had little peace at the beginning in our new apartment. We had hardly moved in when my mother broke her arm out on the street. We didn't have any money, were not yet recognized as refugees, and did not know where to go for medical treatment. Heinz Galinski arranged for her to be treated in the Jewish hospital. He exclaimed jokingly, "You are hardly here and we have already zores [trouble] from you." It was terrible for me in the night to be in bed with my mother and her cast.

Just a few weeks after our arrival, practically all leading representatives of the Jewish Communities escaped from the East. In January, the chairman of the Dresden Jewish Community, Leon Löwenkopf, escaped. Around the same time, the Jewish Community leaders from Leipzig and Erfurt came to the West. Even Jule Meyer, the chairman of the East Berlin Community and a Member of Parliament, defected to the West. Many Jews who remained experienced repressive measures. For example, as a result of pressure from the Party, the historian Helmut Eschwege, who was active in the Dresden Jewish Community, had to leave his position as department head in the Museum for German History. This was one of the concrete results of the "lessons from the trial against the conspiracy centered around Slansky," in the language of the Central Committee of the SED. As they let Eschwege know unofficially, his activities in the Jewish Community, his reading of Yiddish newspapers, and the fact that he had emigrated to Palestine during the Third Reich, among other things, were decisive for his dismissal. When Stalin died in March 1953, the greatest fear subsided for a time, but by then practically the entire leadership of the Jewish Communities was already in the West. Jewish activity in East Germany, already modest in the extreme, would never recuperate from this loss.

15

Arrival in the West

In order to get the papers for a permanent stay in West Berlin, we needed an official statement from the Office of Free Lawyers that we had come to the West due to such political reasons as "endangered in body or soul." This meant, first of all, filling out countless forms affirming that we had never engaged in Communist activities. They were afraid of spies infiltrating the West from East Germany. At least twice a week we had to visit that office, where there was always a huge gaggle of people. Among those waiting, we met Leon Löwenkopf and Jule Meyer again. Different officials interrogated us thoroughly, not once, but week after week. What was the political reason for our escape? Were we members of a Communist party? And so on. Finally we received official recognition and an identification card for displaced persons and refugees. My parents received a pension given as reparation to those persecuted by the Nazis. We could move out from the cramped conditions of our single room and afford a small apartment in the Tempelhof district. I still had acquaintances from Dresden in West Berlin whom I met regularly. In the spring of 1953, I received, through the mediation of some friends, a letter with a picture of a handsome young man who was originally from Poland and who had suffered that which we had been spared: five years of life in a ghetto and concentration camp. He had lost his parents and two siblings, and other family members of his perished in Auschwitz. After the war he had ended up, like many "Displaced Persons," in Bavaria, and he only wanted to remain a couple of months in Germany. Two of his sisters who also had survived the concentration camps emigrated in the late 1940s to California, and the brother was supposed to follow; he only wanted to wrap up the business affairs of the sisters. That took more time than planned. He was not completely healthy after all the difficult years, and he needed frequent rest. One year after the other passed. The sisters with their families waited patiently. Trained as a librarian, the brother gradually established a new life for himself in the small Bavarian city of Weiden. In California his sisters also succeeded in starting a new life, one they would not have even dared to dream about before.

We met each other in Nuremberg and spent a couple of days there. From then on, everything went very fast. Georg Hermann,[1] who characterized so accurately the Berlin Jewish ambience of the nineteenth century, would have written, "And everything happened as it had to happen." On June 16, 1953, we married, and ten months later our first son was born.

My parents got along very well with my husband, but having grown up in Dresden and now living in Berlin, they did not much fancy our provincial little Bavarian town. But they visited us frequently and loved their grandson very much. After all the terrible years we had been through, we were very happy that they had survived and could see this. Unfortunately, my father died in 1956, ironically enough during a visit to our home, and now he is buried here. My mother lived a few more years in Berlin and then she moved into our house. She lived to see her second grandchild, and both children were her pride and joy. We were a very normal family. We were exactly what would not have been allowed to happen according to the program of the Nazis. In 1980 my mother died, on February 13, the anniversary of the bombardment of Dresden. She was buried in the Jewish cemetery of Weiden. Religion, which had not separated my parents in life, divorced them in death. After they had fought together, suffered together, and had sustained each other morally, they, who had been expelled from their home after the liberation, found eternal peace in the same city, but in different cemeteries.

It had been my mother's fondest wish to return for one more visit to Dresden. In her last years of life—she almost turned ninety—she was a little bit confused and even went once to the train station to go "home." That was not, of course, so simple before the fall of the Wall. She did not live to see that and the other political changes in the East. I myself undertook my first journey back with my family, shortly after mother's death, in 1981. At that time, I thought I was seeing my hometown for the last time; the preparations for the trip were so depressing. The West Germans suggested we request a second passport, because our current passports with the stamps from Israel could make it more difficult to obtain an East German visa. Then came the locked doors in the "interzonal train" and the guard dogs at the border station. This could not fail to evoke bitter associations with the past. Then the cityscape of Dresden, with the terribly deformed Prager Strasse, did nothing to help resurrect any positive memories from my childhood. In the Alaunstrasse I found the property where our movie theatre had stood: a squalid square with a sausage shanty. Nevertheless, the old familiar streets, the Mendelssohnallee with the house in which I grew up, the school, the parks Waldpark and Grosser Garten, the Blaues Wunder bridge, Pillnitz castle, the Elbe River—to see all these was worth it in the end. Thus, since the collapse of East Germany, I visit Dresden regularly, not only because of pleasure and nostalgia, but also to do something more important: to tell young people about my experiences in the Third Reich. I have done it in several schools and have always perceived it as a very positive experience. Now I have also been invited to my former school, a prospect that makes me a bit nervous. With joy and also with a little bit of satisfaction I was able to attend the laying of the foundation stone of the new synagogue. Thanks to the invitations from the city of Dresden to its former Jewish fellow citizens, invitations that are now extended annually, I have met some of my school friends again. Also, due to the efforts of the Christian-Jewish society and the initiative Hatikva (hope) and the City, much has been done during the past few years to help people gain a better understanding of the past. Nevertheless, I am accompanied by mixed feelings every time I go "home" again, go for a walk in the garden of my childhood and see the old trees on which I climbed as a child. I am glad that I have been allowed to live to see all that, and still I know: The people from whom "my Dresden" was made have not returned.

Notes

Chapter 1

1. The yellow star, inscribed with the word "Jude," has become a symbol of Nazi persecution of the Jews. This Jewish badge was introduced in September 1941. Henny Brenner provides more detailed information in chapter 8.

2. In August 1938 Jews had to appear at the passport agencies, and female Jews received the additional name "Sara"; males were given the additional name "Israel." See chapter 7.

Chapter 2

1. Today capital of Belarus.

2. Dresden was well known for its tobacco industry. "Tailors" custom cut the tobacco for trade.

3. Papirossi cigarettes have no filter and have a high tar content. Before World War II, papirossi cigarettes were practically all that were available to Russian smokers, and the Russian–Jewish immigrants working in the tobacco trade still made the papirossi cigarettes by hand.

4. A somavar or samovar is literally a "self-brewer." It is a metal container traditionally used by some Slavic and mid-eastern nations to heat and boil water and to make tea.

5. Dresdner Bank was established in 1872 in Dresden, and served as one of the major regional banks in central Germany. In 1881 the bank opened a branch in Berlin, and in 1885 it opened its first international branch in London. By 1900, Dresdner Bank was one of the most important banks in Germany and had the largest German branch network.

6. A "Galician Jew" was someone from the Austro-Hungarian province of Galicia, inhabited by German-speaking settlers, whose territory covered an area that is today partly in Poland and partly in the Ukraine.

7. I will keep the term "Strasse" (in German: Straße = street).

8. The Nuremberg Race Laws, or as they became commonly known, Nuremberg Laws from 1935 were denaturalization laws passed by Nazi Germany which excluded Jews from Reich citizenship. The laws did not define a Jew as someone belonging to the Jewish religious community. Anyone who descended from three or four Jewish grandparents was classified as a Jew. Henny Brenner, with two Jewish grandparents, was classified as a crossbreed, a *Mischling,* of "mixed blood." These laws provided the pseudoscientific basis for discrimination against people they classified as Jews. The laws also forbade Jews from marrying persons of "German or related blood," or having extramarital sexual relations with them.

9. Large lake in the southwest of Berlin, which is frequented by the Berliners primarily during the summer months.

10. One of the largest and most exquisite department stores in Berlin.

11.These are street addresses. A "Gasse" is an alley, as in Große Brüdergasse; a "Platz" is a square.

12. Literal translation: mill of the dead.

13. The Charité is today the largest university hospital in Europe and has always been the best known hospital in Berlin. Many famous physicians and scientists worked at the Charité.

14. Today in Poland; formerly the province of Prussia, Germany.

15. Richard Tauber (1891–1948): An Austrian tenor and one of the greatest singers of the twentieth century, who due to his Jewish ancestry left Nazi Germany in 1933 and Austria in 1938; he spent the Nazi period in exile in the United Kingdom.

16. Wilhelm Furtwängler (1886–1954): A German conductor and composer, Furtwängler was appointed director of some of the major German orchestras, among them the Berlin Philharmonic Orchestra (1923). His relationship with the Nazi Party led to much controversy. He remained in Germany during the Nazi period as one of the most favored conductors in Germany, but claimed that he was never a supporter of the Nazi leadership. Furtwängler was cleared of charges during his denazification trial, but it was not until 1952 that he resumed his post as principal conductor of the Berlin Philharmonic.

17. Baldur von Schirach (1907–1974): A Nazi youth leader, head of the Hitler Youth, and later Reich Governor of Vienna. He was convicted of being a war criminal during the Nuremberg trials and was sentenced to and served twenty years in prison.

CHAPTER 3

1. Notable German Jewish family. Moses Mendelssohn (1729–1786) was a German Jewish philosopher and representative of the Enlightenment. His

grandson Felix Mendelssohn Bartholdy was a famous composer and conductor of the Romantic period.

2. Sebastian Kneipp (1821–1897): A priest and the founder of naturopathic medicine. Kneipp was a proponent of an entire system of healing which included hydrotherapy, herbalism, exercise, nutrition, and spirituality.

3. A pond in the middle of Grosser Garten.

4. Historic district and suburb of Dresden.

5. Literally: Park in the Forest.

CHAPTER 4

1. The "Blue Wonder" bridge or Loschwitz Bridge is a bridge over the Elbe River connecting the exclusive villa districts Dresden-Blasewitz with Dresden-Loschwitz.

CHAPTER 5

1. Dresden's busiest shopping street with exclusive stores and restaurants. During the bombing attacks Prager Strasse was also reduced to rubble and was rebuilt according to Socialist urban planning in the sixties and seventies.

2. The German "Ratskeller" are restaurants on the street level or in the basements of the city halls, where the city councilmen used to eat. These restaurants generally serve local food and are favored by the middle class.

CHAPTER 6

1. The Semperoper, the opera house in Dresden, is one of the most famous opera houses in the world. Built by Dresden architect Gottfried Semper in 1841 and destroyed by Allied bombings, it was rebuilt in 1985.

2. A weekly Nazi newspaper that served the Nazi propaganda machine and as a consequence was deeply antisemitic.

3. BDM (Bund Deutscher Mädel), The League of German Girls was the only female youth organization in Nazi Germany and a branch of the Hitler Youth.

4. The SS (Schutzstaffel), the Shield Squadron was originally a paramilitary unit. Under the leadership of Heinrich Himmler it grew between 1929 and 1945 into Hitler's powerful elite police and military unit, parallel to and not always in consensus with the army, the *Wehrmacht*. Built upon racist ideology, the SS was responsible for innumerable crimes against humanity.

5. On November 7, 1938 Herschel Grynszpan, who was Jewish, assassinated Ernst vom Rath, a minor official at the German embassy in Paris.

6. Henny Brenner is referring to the expulsion of around 15,000 Polish Jews, who in October 1938 had been forced across the Silesian border at Zbaszyn.

CHAPTER 7

1. The Nazis organized pogroms against German Jews throughout Germany and parts of Austria on the night of November 9, 1938, commonly known as the "Night of the Broken Glass," or "Kristallnacht." Jewish homes, shops, and businesses were destroyed in numerous German towns and cities, and Jewish synagogues were destroyed and set on fire all over Germany. German Jews were beaten, some to death; others were arrested and sent to concentration camps.

2. Concentration camp outside of Weimar, Germany.

3. SA (Sturmabteilung), often translated as "Stormtroopers," functioned as a paramilitary organization of the Nazi party. The SA played a major role in bringing Hitler to power.

CHAPTER 8

1. Victor Klemperer, *I Will Bear Witness: A Diary of the Nazi Years 1942–1945*, translated by Martin Chalmers, New York: Random House, 1999, 47.

2. A famous Dresden landmark, the Carola bridge over the Elbe River connects the Dresden old city (Altstadt) with the Dresden new city (Neustadt).

3. Organization Todt refers to an organization founded in 1938 by the Nazi Fritz Todt, Minister of the Reich for Armament and Amunition (Reichsminister für Bewaffnung und Munition), who died in an airplane accident in 1942.

CHAPTER 9

1. The German "peinlich" means "embarrassing." The pronunciation in Saxon dialect for "peinlich" is "beinlich." The director's name was "Beinlich." Werner Lang talks about the embarrassing incident with a change in the pronunciation of the first letter from p to b, referring both to the director's last name and to the embarrassing episode.

2. The diaries, filling two large volumes, were first published in Germany under the title *Ich will Zeugnis ablegen bis zum letzten: Tagebücher 1933–1945*, Berlin: Aufbau Verlag, 1995. For the translation in English by Martin Chalmers see Chapter 8, note 1. Victor Klemperer was a professor of Romance

Languages at the Technical University of Dresden. Like Brenner's mother, he had escaped deportation to the death camps only due to the fact that he was married to an "Aryan" spouse. Klemperer, who stayed in Germany and had intended to be the "cultural historian for the present catastrophe" (10 January 1942), recorded in his "Diaries 1933–1945" the horrors of Nazism and the ruin it brought for Germany. After their publication the diaries became a bestseller due to their literary quality and their political appeal. Klemperer's interest in the corrupted language of totalitarianism also made the diaries and his book *Lingua Tertii Imperii* (1947) an important source for linguists and literary scholars.

3. Eva Klemperer, a former concert pianist, was not Jewish. By sharing all of her husband's humiliations, her help was crucial in saving Victor Klemperer from the death camps. His diaries give testimony to their love and close partnership during a time of fear, hardship, and terror.

CHAPTER 10

1. The German name for the town Terezín, today in the Czech Republic, formerly a military fortress and garrison town. The Nazis used the fortress as a Gestapo prison, and the fortress town functioned as a ghetto and transit camp on the way to extermination camps.

CHAPTER 12

1. Sound of a name the Russian soldiers used for "girl."
2. The full German name was: Vereinigung der Verfolgten des Naziregimes.
3. Sozialistische Einheitspartei Deutschlands.
4. An island in the Baltic Sea, today at the border of Germany and Poland.
5. Town in the mountainous region called *Erzgebirge* (Eastern Ore Mountains) south of Dresden.
6. A Jewish holiday celebrated in the spring. One of the traditional foods served during Purim are triangular pastries called homentashn (Haman's pockets).

CHAPTER 14

1. On 20 November 1952 Rudolf Slansky, General Secretary of the Communist Party in Czechoslovakia, and thirteen other communist leaders or bu-

reaucrats, eleven of them Jews, were convicted and later executed. Slansky became a prominent example of the purges of Jews from the leadership of Communist parties in Eastern Europe.

2. This was the planned show trial of Paul Merker (1894–1969), a leading East German, non-Jewish communist. Merker was charged with acting as an American-Zionist agent. He was arrested in 1952 in connection with the Slansky trials and in 1955 was sentenced to eight years in a high security prison for espionage.

3. Heinz Galinski (1912–1992) was chairman of the Jewish Community in Berlin from 1949–1992, and from 1988 until his death in 1992 he was head of the Central Council of the Jews in Germany.

CHAPTER 15

1. Georg Hermann (1871–1943), a German-Jewish author who either died during his transport to Auschwitz or was murdered in Auschwitz.

Index

Index